CONTROL OF RICE ROOT KNOT NEMATODE BY ESSENTIAL OIL OF INDIGENOUS MEDICINAL PLANTS OF MANIPUR

Dr. Laishram Joymati Devi
Associate Professor (Zoology)
Department of Zoology
P.G. Center, D.M. College of Sciences,
Imphal, Manipur

ISBN 979-8-88546-735-3

Contents

Acknowledgements

I would like to express my special thanks of gratitude and indebtedness to The Science and Engineering Research Board (SERB), Department of Science and Technology, Government of India *for their valuable financial contribution and encouragement for undergoing the Research project a grand success.*

Gratefulness is extended to the Principal, D.M. College of Science, Imphal for providing necessary laboratory and infrastructure facilities. Also, I would like to express my special thanks of gratitude to my Research Scholars for their valuable contribution in field survey works and laboratory data collection during the course of investigation works.

Also, I would like to thank my daughter Dr. H. Sushmita Devi, son H. Khaushal Kumar Singh and husband H. Manoj kumar Singh who helped and motivated me a lot in making this project unique and bring out this book a grand success.

At last but not in least, I would like to thank everyone who helped to work on this project.

(Dr. L. Joymati Devi)
Associate Professor (Zoology)
D.M. College of Science, Imphal

Introduction

Manipur is situated in the north eastern border of India. It has two different regions, one is hilly region and another is central valley region. The state covers an area of 22, 356 sq. km of which the hilly region covers about 91.75% while the remaining 8.25% of the total geographical area constitutes the central valley region. It lies between 23^0 51'N to 25^0 41'N latitudes and 93^0 2'E to 94^0 47'E longitudes. Two different types of climatic conditions are found in this state according to altitude topography and direction of prevailing wind system. The cool temperate climate prevails in the hilly areas whereas the tropical monsoon type of climate prevails in the valley areas. The average minimum temperature of this state is 3^0 C, the maximum temperature is 30^0 C and the rainfall is about 2077 mm per annum. The type of soil found in the hilly area is red, stoney, gravelly or heavy soil with a soil P^H ranging from 5-6 i.e. acidic in nature and in the plain areas it ranges from sandy loam to clay loam with soil P^H varying from 6.5 to 8.1.

Meloidogyne graminicola is an important pest of several economically useful rice crops. It is an obligate endoparasitic nematode. The root knot nematodes have a wide range of hosts. Due to the root knot nematodes particularly *M. graminicola* it is very difficult and sometime impossible to grow normally rice plant and infected in their production. The disease complex caused by these nematodes is one of the most lethal that is known currently.

In India work on plant nematology started with the report of root knot on tea plant by Barber (1901) from Munnar, Kerala, India. Many Indian workers like Butter (1913), Dastur (1936), Siddiqi (1959, 1961, 1963, 1964, 1965, 1969, 1978, 1986). Jairajpuri (1962, 1964, 1965, 1966, 1967, 1968, 1970), Baqri et.al., (1978), Bajaj and Jairajpuri (1979), Phukan and Sanwal (1979, 1980, 1980a) etc. have made significant contribution in nematology specially in the taxonomical aspect.

Root knot nematode management has been a long practice. Records shown that management in India started with scientist like Singh (1965) on tomato with carrot cake. But in Manipur management on root knot nematode begain recently by Joymati et.al. (1996) against *M. incognita* infecting *V. faba* with aqueous extracts of *P. javanica*. Recently Joymati and Thoithoi (2010) reported rice root knot nematode from Manipur for first time.

Keeping this in view the present work has been taken up to investigate about the following objectives.

1st Year

i. Survey on incidence of rice root knot nematode on different rice fields of Manipur.
ii. Identification of plants for new host record for rice root knot nematode if discovered.
iii. Identification of different species of root knot nematode found in Manipur.

2nd Year

i. Host range studies of rice root knot nematode in different varieties of rice.
ii. Collection of medicinal plants from different localities and districts of Manipur.
iii. Preparation of Oil extracts from different medicinal plants.
iv. Management studies will be started after testing their properties against rice root knot nematode under laboratory condition.

3rd Year

i. Effect of different oil extracts against egg hatching, larval mortality and penetration of *Meloidogyne graminicola* in vitro.

ii. Efficacy of oil extracts against rice root knot nematode on different varieties of rice under pot experiment.

iii. The most effective oil extracts will try to apply at field condition.

iv. Transfer of technology to the farmers.

The present works has been divided into two chapters.

Chapter 1 Ecological studies

1.1 Survey on incidence of rice root knot nematode on different rice fields of Manipur

1.2 Identification of different species of root knot nematode found in Manipur

1.3 Host range studies of rice root knot nematode in different varieties of rice.

Chapter 2 Management studies

2.1 Collection of 10 different medicinal plants from different localities in plain districts of Manipur.

2.2 Preparation of different essential oil extracts from the collected medicinal plants.

2.3 Management

Laboratory Condition

a. Evaluation of essential oil extracts obtained from the 10 selected medicinal plants against egg hatching and larval mortality of *M. graminicola*.

Pot Experiment

b. Efficacy of essential oil extracts of medicinal plants against rice root knot nematode *Meloidogyne graminicala* in pots.

c. Evaluation of essential oils of medicinal plants against rice root knot pest in Manipur

d. One day training program for transfer of technology to the farmers.

General Methodology

1. Collection of soil samples

Soil samples were collected from around the roots of vegetables, medicinal and wild plants from different parts of Manipur. Soil samples were collected from a depth of 10 to 30 cm discarding the top layer. The collected soil samples were mixed thoroughly and from this bulk samples, about 500g of soils was taken as the representative soil samples, were put into the polythene bags and relevant information with respect to the host plant, locality, date of collection, etc were noted, then the collected soil samples were brought to the laboratory for further study.

2. Processing of Soil Samples.

The collected soil samples were processed for the extraction of nematode by Cobb's (1918) sieving and decanting method followed by modified Baermann's funnel technique. For this 500 ml beaker of soil was put in a plastic bucket after a thorough breakage of the big chunks, tap water is filled upto half level of the bucket and gently stirred with hand, breaking all the bigger soil clods. Some more water was added thereby making all the soil free nematodes to float in the aliquot. After standing the suspension for a few seconds, the heavy soil particles settled down. The whole aliquot was then passed through a 350 mesh sieve slowly using tap water for washing and the catch was collected in a beaker. It was then passed through a strainer already lined with double layer tissue paper. After that, the strainer was put into the Baermann's funnel, already filled with clean filter water in such a way that the strainer is half dipped into the water, the nematode suspension collected at the lower portion of the funnel is taken out by opening the clip.

3. Killing and fixing

Suspension collected was poured into a collecting tube and allowed to settle at the bottom by standing for 4-5 hours and the excess water was decanted out as far as possible and the remaining suspension was poured into a cavity block. After sucking out the excess water, the nematodes were killed and fixed in warm F.A. (3:1). Thus fixed nematodes were stored in cavity blocks or glass vials for longer preservation.

4. Dehydration

After one day or more 10-20 fixed nematodes representing each genus contained in the sample were transferred into G.A. (Glycerine 5 parts: Alcohol 95 parts) and kept in a desiccators at room temperature for about two to three weeks for complete dehydration.

5. Mounting and sealing

The dehydrated nematodes were mounted in anhydrous glycerine on glass slides and the desired nematode already dehydrated was put into it. Three pieces of glass wool of suitable thickness were also placed on the slides in a triangular way. Then a cover slip was placed over it. The excess amount of glycerin from the edge of the cover slip was blotted out. Finally, the edge of the cover slip were sealed with nail polish.

6. Measurements, Drawing and Photographs

De man's (1884) formula was used for denoting the dimensions of the nematodes. Measurements were taken using an ocular micrometer under a compound microscope. All the necessary diagrams were drawn with the help of camera lucida. A canon camera was used for taking the photographs.

7. Collection of root samples

Root samples from different localities were collected for examination of infestation by *M. graminicola* on rice plants in four plain district of in Manipur. The survey work ere conducted from July 2012 upto October

2014. Five to ten root samples were collected at random from different fields in a locality in polythene bags. Root samples were thoroughly wash under tap water and were examined for presence of galls.

8. Publication

For the sake of authenticity, some of the research findings have already been sent for publication, with the permission of the authorities concerned. With a view to maintain uniformity and to have a glimpse of the efficiency effects of the extracts of different medicinal plants, on nematode pest-management, the published findings are again reproduced here by incorporating them in the relevant chapters.

9. Other experimental methodology

Necessary methodology of the experiments done are provided in the relevant chapters.

Chapter - 1

Ecological Studies

1.1 Survey on incidence of rice root knot nematode on different rice fields of Manipur

Introduction

Root knot nematodes (*Meloidogyne* species) infecting different economically important crops are one of the most widely spread pathogens limiting world agricultural productivity. Almost all of the plants that account for the majority of the world's food supply are susceptible to this group of pathogens (Sasser et. al. 1982; Taylor et. al, 1982), Sasser (1980) and Sasser & Carter (1982) estimated that in areas where root knot nematodes were not controlled, average crop yield loss was about 25 percent with damage in individual fields ranging as high as 60 percent. The occurrence of *Meloidogyne speciesa* in different parts of India has been reported by many workers, Bhatti and Dahiya (1977); Sen and Dasgupta (1975) and (1977); Trivedi and Datta (1986); Verma and Singh (1983); Raveendran and Nadakal (1975); Das, Mishra and Mahanty (1979); Haseeb and Pandey (1987). Bhatti and Jain (1977) and Jain et. al. (1986) also worked out yield losses of different crops infecting *M. incognita* in Haryana but rather scanty. Thus the study of distribution and infestation pattern of *Meloidogyne sp.* is primary importance for planning management strategies of root knot nematode in different parts of the country. Khan and Khan (1996) observed about 50 percent root knot disease incidence on different vegetable crops in Merut districts of U.P. India and recorded 36% above root samples were infested with root knot nematodes. To investigate the effect and their number of association with other plant parasitic nematodes infecting many crops, the study was being made, which will be of useful information in the nematode management program. Queneherve et. al. (1995) investigated host status of some weeds to *Meloidogyne* spp., *Pratylenchus* spp., *Helicotylenchus* spp. and *Rotylenchulus* reniformis associated with vegetable cultivated in Polytunnels in Martinique for 33 weed species and observed that the most frequently encountered nematodes were *Rotylenchulus* reniformis followed by four species of *Meloidogyne, Helicotylenchus* and *Pratylenchus* and four weed species were found to be nematode free. Khan (2000) investigated occurrence of root knot nematode *M. incognita* and other plant parasitic nematodes, *Pratylenchus pratensis, Xihinema bergeri, Hoplolaimus indicus, Merlinius nizamii, Helicotylenchus dihystera* and *Tylenchorhynchus mashhoodi* were commonly occurring nematodes species on Kiwi fruit (Actinidia delicious Chev.) in Himachal Pradesh. Das and Das (2000) also reported prevalence of 140 infected root samples of tomato, brinjal, cabbage, French bean, okra and papaya with root-knot Nematodes in Assam and Arunachal Pradesh, Bhagawati and Bora (2001) reported a new record on root knot nematode infecting *Amaranthus blitum* in Assam. Dhanachand (1982) reported *M. incognita* from tomato, *Lycopersicon esculentum L.* grown in Waithou Hill, Thoubal.

Recently, in Manipur Joymati and Thoithoi 2010 reported rice root knot nematode from Manipur. This information, even though vital, is still meager. Keeping in this view the present investigation has been taken up to evaluate their distribution and infestation pattern andcontrol of rice root knot nematode in Manipur which provide information on the sources of inoculums and off season biology to the nematode which can be advantageously utilized for their management.

1.2 Identification of detected root knot nematode upto their species level

Meloidogyne spp belongs to family Heteroderidae. The root knot nematode was first named by Cornu 1879 in France. White Head

1968 reviewed the genus *Meloidogyne* and confirmed the distinctive morphological charactcrs of 23 spccics of *Meloidogyne*. In this present studies many specimen of root knot nematode were found and the specimen were identified as *Meloidogyne incognita* and *Meloidogyne graminicola* based on the perennial cuticular pattern of gravid female. The detailed dimensions and description with suitable illustrations are provided.

Two species of root knot species were discovered during this investigation report.

***Meloidogyne incognita* (Kofoid and White, 1919) Chitwood, 1949.**

Dimensions

Female (32)

L = 0.53-0.81 (0.69) mm; neck length = 120.5-215.0 (167.7) mm; greatest breadth = 447.0-584.5 (506.5) mm; head to base of median oesophagial bulb = 81.5-137.5 (114.5) mm; medianbulb = 51.5-103.0 (77.5) mm long x 34.5-68.5 (51.6) mm broad; stylet = 13.0-13.5 (13.5) mm; widthof stylt base = 6.0mm; orifice of dorsal oesophageal gland = 3.0 mm from stylet base.

Male (15)

L = 1.15-1.22 (1.15) mm; breadth = 28.5-41.5 (35.0) mm; a = 29.5-39.5934.5); head length = 4.5-5.5 (5.0) mm; head width = 9.5-12.5 (11.0) mm, stylet = 16.0-20.0 (18.5) mm; width of stylet base = 3.0-4.0 (3.5) mm; orifice of dorsal gland = 1.5mm from stylet base; T = 60.5-66.5 mm; spicules = 20.5-32.5 (26.5) mm; gubernaculums = 7.0-9.5 (8.5) mm.

Second stage juveniles (25)

L = 0.35 0.57 (0.47) mm; brcadth = 13.0-17.0 (25.0) mm; a = 27.5-38.0 (31.5); b = 3.0-3.5; b^1 = 6.5 - 9.0 (7.5); stylet = 10.5-13.0 (11.5) mm; orifice of dorsal gland = 3.0mm behind stylet base; tail length = 47.5-71.0 (61.5) mm, 7.0-8.7 (7.5); ABD = 8.5-10.0 (10.0) mm.

Eggs (20)

Length = 74.0-86.0 (78.5) mm; ratio of length to breadth = 2.1-2.4 (2.20); eggs are elongated oblong.

Remark

Meloidogyne incognita is widely distributed in Manipur along with a wide range of host. The measurements and morphological characters of the present populations are similar with those dimensions given by Orton (1973), Eisenback (1985), Hirchmann (1985), Jairajpuri and Baqri (1991). But the present male specimens have slightly shorter stylet and gubernaculums..

***Meloidogyne graminicola*, (Golden and Birchfield, 1965):**

Kingdom: Metazoa

- **Phylum: Nematoda**
- **Family: Meloidogynidae**
- **Genus: Meloidogyne**
- **Species: *Meloidogyne graminicola***

Measurements (After Golden and Birchfield, 1965)

20 females: L = 0.445-0.764 (0.573) mm; width = 0.274-0.518 (0.419) mm; a =. 2-1.8 (1.37); stylet = 10.44-11.20 (11.08) µm. 20 males: L = 1.120-1.228 (1.222) mm; a = 72.7-205.0 (117.4); length of oesophagus (anterior end to base of oesophagus) = 196.0-250.0 (222.0) µm; stylet = 16.88-17.31 (16.8) µm. 20 second-stage juveniles: L = 0.413-0.474 (0.441) mm; a = 21.3-26.3 (24.8); b = 2.8-4.1 (3.2); c = 5.4-6.4 (6.2); stylet = 11.10-12.12 (11.38) µm. 20 eggs: L = 94-103 (99) µm; width = 41-45 (44) µm.

Perineal patterns:

Oval or egg-shaped, no lateral line, the cuticular striae are smooth, thick strand in the outer region of the oval pattern. Dorsal to the vulva, the striae anastomose into a tetragonal or pyramidal web that converges at the tail terminus. A semicircular whorl consisting of two to three striae is present at each corner of the vulvar slit.

Female Description (after Mulk, 1976)

Pearly white, globular to pear-shaped with small neck; cuticle distinctly annulated but often marked with irregular punctations. Lip region smooth, anteriorly flattened, not distinctly set off from neck, with inconspicuous framework. Stylet slender and delicate; knobs rounded with posteriorly sloping anterior margins. Orifice of dorsal oesophageal gland 3.2 (2.8-3.9) µm behind stylet base. Excretory pore conspicuous, anterior to median oesophageal bulb, more than one stylet length posterior to stylet knobs and 7-16 annules behind lip region. Procorpus elongate cylindrical; median oesophageal bulb large, situated in the hind part of the neck, highly muscular, rounded to hemispheroid, 20-23 µm long and 10-12 µm wide with strongly cuticularized valve in the middle; isthmus short and narrow; three oesophageal glands, each with a prominent nucleus, extend ventrally and ventro-laterally over the intestine. Nerve ring obscure.

Ovaries two, well developed, convoluted, filling body cavity and overlying the intestine; uterus with several eggs. Six large radially arranged, uninucleate rectal glands with prominent nuclei, surround the rectum. Posterior cuticular pattern (= perineal pattern) dorso-ventrally oval, sometimes almost circular; dorsal arch low with smooth striae; tail tip marked with prominent, coarse, fairly well separated and disorganized striae, forming an irregular tail whorl; sometimes a few lines converge at either end of vulva. Lateral fields obscure or absent. A few well-marked, irregular, short, zig-zag striae, distinct from the rest and interrupting the general pattern, distinguish it from other species. Phasmids minute, rather close together; distance between the phasmids about two-thirds the length of the vulva. Distance from anus to vulva about 2.5-3.0 times the distance between anus and level of phasmids.

Male

Body cylindrical, vermiform, tapering more towards anterior than posterior extremity. Cuticle prominently annulated. Annules about 2.1-2.5 µm apart near mid-body. Lip region continuous with body or slightly offset by a constriction, nearly flat anteriorly, 3.5-4.0 µm high and 8.5-9.0 µm wide, consisting of a prominent labial annule followed by 1 or sometimes 2 wide post-labials. Cephalic framework conspicuously sclerotized. Stylet fairly strong with rounded posteriorly sloping knobs, 3.5-4.0 µm across; anterior conical part of stylet about 50% of the whole length. Orifice of the dorsal oesophageal gland 3.5-4.8 µm (2.80-3.92 µm according to Golden and Birchfield, 1965) from base of stylet. Anterior and posterior cephalids at about 2nd and 7th annules behind lip region. Excretory pore distinct, 51-64 annules behind lip region (about 0-7 annules posterior to nerve ring). Hemizonid 1-2 annules wide, 1-3 annules anterior to the excretory pore. Hemizonion a few annules behind excretory pore but inconspicuous. Procorpus elongate, cylindrical, wider than isthmus. Median oesophageal bulb hemispheroid to fusiform with strongly cuticularized valve in the middle. Isthmus, a narrow tube, encircled by nerve ring near middle; three oesophageal glands forming a compact lobe overlie intestine ventrally and ventro-laterally. Lateral fields 7.7 (6.2-9.5) µm wide or about one quarter of body-width, marked with 4 incisures in young and 8 in large and old specimens, near mid-body. Outer incisures crenate and outer bands areolated at extremities. Testis single, outstretched, sometimes reflexed anteriorly. Spicules arcuate or slightly bent ventrally near middle, 28.1 (27.4-29.1) µm long medially. Gubernaculum rod-shaped 6.1 (5.6-6.7) µm long. Tail 11.1 (6.2-15.1) µm wide with smooth terminus. Phasmids small, postanal, located near middle of tail.

Second-stage juveniles.

Body cylindrical, vermiform, tapering towards posterior extremity. Cuticle finely marked with distinct transverse striae, about 1 µm apart near mid-body. Lip region continuous with body, weakly sclerotized, marked with 3 faint post-labial annules. Stylet delicate with posteriorly sloping rounded knobs. Orifice of dorsal oesophageal gland 2.8 (2.8-3.4) µm from base of stylet. Excretory pore at level of nerve ring or slightly behind. Hemizonid just anterior to excretory pore. Median oesophageal bulb rounded, almost spherical, with prominent refractive valve. Lateral fields with 3 incisures, occupying one-quarter to one-third of body width near middle. Outer incisures finely crenate. Tail 70.9 (67.0-76.0) µm long, including the irregularly annulated posterior hyaline portion, which is 17.9 (14.0-21.2) µm long and 4-5 times as long as the anal body width. Tail terminus rounded, often slightly clavate.

Biology and Ecology

M. graminicola is found in upland soils, shallow flooded soils and deep flooded soils. It is well adapted to flooded conditions and can survive in waterlogged soil as eggs in egg masses or as juveniles for long periods. Numbers of *M. graminicola* decline rapidly after 4 months but some egg masses can remain viable for at least 14 months in waterlogged soil (Roy, 1982). *M. graminicola* can survive in soil flooded to a depth of 1 m for at least 5 months (Bridge and Page, 1982), it cannot invade rice in flooded conditions but quickly invades when infested soils are drained (Manser, 1968). All *Meloidogyne* spp. can be spread in soil and on seedlings of other crop hosts planted to a field. Because *M. oryzae* and, especially, *M. graminicola* are found in flooded rice there is the additional danger of dissemination in irrigation and run-off water.

Life Cycle

M. graminicola has a very short life cycle on rice of less than 19 days at temperatures of 22-29°C, and an isolate from the USA completed its cycle in 23-27 days at 26°C (Yik and Birchfield, 1979). In India the life cycle of *M. graminicola* is reported to be 26-51 days, depending on time of year (Rao and Israel, 1973).

Infective, second-stage juveniles of *M. graminicola* invade rice roots in upland conditions just behind the root tip (Buangsuwon et al., 1971; Rao and Israel, 1973). Females develop within the root and eggs are mainly laid in the cortex (Roy, 1976a). Juveniles can remain in the maternal gall or migrate intercellularly through the aerenchymatous tissues of the cortex to new feeding sites within the same root (Bridge and Page, 1982). This behaviour appears to be an adaptation by *M. graminicola* to flooded conditions enabling it to continue multiplying within the host tissues even when roots are deeply covered by water. Juveniles that migrate from rice roots in flooded soil cannot re-invade.

1.3 Host range studies of rice root knot nematode in different varieties of rice

Rice (*Oryza sativa L.*) is an important staple food crop for majority of human population in the world in general and in Asia in particular. In India, rice occupies more than one quarters of the cropped area and contribute between 40-43 % of total food grain *Meloidogyne graminicola,* the root knot nematode is an obligate parasite of rice, *Oryza sativa.* Yield loses upto 50% might be incurred due to severe infestation of *Meloidogyne graminicola* in upland, rainfed anddirect seeded rice (Lorenzana et.al.1998) under field condition. In pot experiment reduction in grain yield was reported upto 98% (Plowright and Bridge, 1990). The use of resistant cultivars is a low cost and sustainable option for the control of nematodes in the long term which does not imposed unwanted changes in traditional agronomic practices (Amoussou et.al 2004). So, far, efforts to breed rice cultivars resistant to root knot nematode have been limited. However attempts have been made to screen popular varieties (Sampath et.al.1970; Israel and Rao, 1971; Roy 1973) to identify those that are suitable to be cultivated in nematode infested areas. Among the plant parasitic nematodes, root-knot nematodes (*Meloidogyne* spp.) are distributed worldwide and possess a broad host range of economically important crops. They are recognized as causing more economic damage to food crops compared from any other plant parasitic nematode and are ranked first among ten highly pathogenic nematode genera. About2000 plants are susceptible to their infection causing approximately 5% of global crop loss (Hussey and Janssen, 2002). Generally, root-knot nematodes inhabit farm soils with the species of host plants cultivated influencing their distribution. The population of nematodes is mostly found 5 to 30 cm beneath the soil surface. In presence of a suitable host the distribution of *Meloidogyne* in the soil reaches the same as that of crop plant roots. Damage due to the root-knot nematode causes poor growth, decline in the quality and yield of the crop and reduction in the resistance to stressors, such as, drought, diseases, etc. Damaged roots fail to utilize water and fertilizers effectively, leading to additional losses. A high level of root-knot nematode damage can lead to total crop loss. Infections of young plants are lethal, while those in mature plants are responsible for yield reduction. Besides affecting plant health, they also act as vectors of other pathogens (bacteria, fungus, virus), wounding agents, host modifiers, resistance breakers and rhizosphere modifiers. To meet the increasing demands of the ever growing human population, an effective use of available land for increasing production of food and fibre throughout the world has become a necessity. Besides, expensive labor and higher cost of inputs in agriculture are major constraints. Hence, it becomes imperative to control losses due to diseases and pests like nematodes in agriculture production. The basic requirement would be thus to find out the economic importance of the parasites on the basis of population densities and distribution, nature and amount of damage and the losses in yield.

The present investigation was undertaken for screening resistant varieties of rice by screening of some common rice varities cultivated in Manipur was tested against *Meloidogyne graminicola* under tub condition in the Nematology Laboratory D.M. College of Science, P.G. Department of Zoology during July 2012 upto November 2012.

MATERIALS AND METHOD

1.1 Survey on incidence of rice root knot nematode on different rice fields of Manipur

A preliminary survey of rice root knot nematode from July 2012 upto October 2014 was conducted in different four plain districts of Manipur they are Imphal East, Imphal west, Bisnupur and Thoubal Districts. Out of 250 different villages surveyed only 80 localities were selected from the four plain district. The localities of Imphal east are Loijing maya loubuk, Loijing ching maya loukon, Sinam lok loukon, Yumlok loukon,

Checkon loukon, Kanglou loukon, Ikop loukon, Thingel makha loukon, Kharou loukon, Kongon toubi loukon, Nungoi loukon, Huidrom loukon, Sawombung loukon, Hidumbi loukon, Wairikhul loukol, Mani yaiskul loukol, Thamnapokpi loukon, Bamon loukon, and Patlou loukon. The localities of Imphal West are Malom, Maklang, Samurou Kobok loukol, Hiyangthang makha loukol, Meijrao loukol, Kakyai loukol, Mekola loukol, Langpok Loukol, Merakhong Loukol, Lairenjam Loukol, Konthoujam Loukol, Utlou Makha leikai, Phoijing, Nambol, Nambol thongkha, Nambol Sabal Leikai, Maibam Lokpa Ching, Oinam loukol, Erengbam loukol, Yaral Loukol. The villages of Bisnupur districts are Maibam Loukol, Leimaram Lamkhai Loukol, Oinam Loukol, Irengbam Loukol, Keinou thongthak Loukol, Keinou thongkha Loukol, Keinou Maning Loukol,

Keinou Mamang Loukol, Ngaikhong Khun Loukol, Pumphou Loukol, Ngakchoupkpi Loukol, Chingdong Loukol, Bishenpur Maning Loukol, Bishenpur Mamang Loukol, Kwaksiphai Loukol, Khoijuman Loukol, Potsangbam Loukol. The villages of Thoubal districts are Khekman Loukol, Sanggaiyumpham Loukol, Keibung Loukol, Wabgai Loukol, Khangabok Loukol, Serou Loukol, Phundrei Loukol, Kakmayai Loukol, Heirok Loukol, Hiyanglam Loukol, Tentha Loukol, Thounaojam Loukol as shown

in the Table 1.1a, 1.1b, 1.1c, 1.1d.. Diseased field were selected on the basis of above ground symptom of the crops such as wilting, slow growth, stunting and yellowing of leaves. Altogether 800 soil samples were collected as per 10 samples from each field. Along with infected plants, the soil samples were also collected from the rhizospheric region from a depth of 10-15 cm at the rate of one unit sample. Each unit sample was a composit of 20 cores obtained from four corners and center of the field and then proceeded for the extraction of nematode by Cobb's (1918), Sieving and decanting method followed by Bairmann's funnel technique for collecting second stag juvenile. Identification of the species for female were mainly based on the perennial cuticular patterns of gravid female described by Sasser and

Carter (1985). From each infected plants observation on intensity of infection, root knot index on (0-5) scale and number of galls were determined. The collected soil samples were mixed thoroughly and taken and put into the polythene bags and relevant information with respect to the infected host plant, locality, date of collection etc., were noted. The soil samples were processed for the extraction of nematode, for this 500 ml beaker of soil was put in a plastic bucket after a thorough breakage of the chunks, tap water is filled upto half level of the bucket and gently stirred with hand breaking all the bigger soil clods. Some more water was added there by making all the soil free nematodes to float in the aliquot. After standing the suspension for a few seconds, the heavy soil particles settled down. The whole aliquot was then passed through a 350 mesh sieve slowly tap water for washing and the catch was collected in a beaker. It was then passed through a strainer already lined with double layer tissue paper. After that, the strainer was put into the Bairmann's Funnel are already filled with clean filter water in such away that the strainer is half dipped into the water, the nematode suspension collected at the lower portion of the funnel is taken out by opening the clip. Suspension collected was poured into a collecting tube and allowed to settle at the bottom by standing for 4-5 hours and the excess water was decanted out as far as possible and the remaining suspension was poured into a cavity block. After sucking out the excess water, the nematodes were killed and fixed in warm Fatty Acid (3:1).

Thus fixed nematodes were stored in cavity blocks or glass vials for longer preservation. After one day or more 10-20 fixed nematodes representing each genus contained in the sample were transferred into G.S. (Glycerine 5 parts: Alcohol 95 parts) and kept in a desiccators at room temperature for about two to three weeks for complete dehydration.

The dehydrated nematodes were mounted in anhydrous glycerin on glass slides and the desired nematode already dehydrated was put into it. Three pieces of glass wool of suitable thickness were also placed on the slides in a triangular way. Then a cover slip was placed over it. The excess amount of glycerine from the edge of the cover slip was blotted up. Finally, the edge of the cover slip were sealed with nail polish. De man's (1884) for mula was used for denoting the dimensions of the nematodes. Measurements were taken using an ocular micrometer under a compound microscope. Many nematologist proposed different system of classification of nematodes, which created confusions. In order to avoid such problems and for simplicity of reference in this present survey work of nematodes the classification system of Siddiqi (1986) for *Tylenchs* are followed.. Absolute frequency, relative frequency, absolute density, relative density and prominence value of each nematode genus were determined (Norton, 1978) as follows:

$$\text{Absolute Frequency} = \frac{\text{No. of samples containing a species}}{\text{Total no. of sample collected}} \times 100$$

$$\text{Relative Frequency} = \frac{\text{Frequency of species}}{\text{Sum of frequency of all species}} \times 100$$

$$\text{Absolute Density} = \frac{\text{No. of individuals of a species in a sample}}{\text{Volume of sample}} \times 100$$

$$\text{Relative Density} = \frac{\text{No. of individuals of a species in a sample}}{\text{Total of all individual in a sample}} \times 100$$

$$\text{Prominence value} = \text{Density X} \sqrt{\text{frequency}}/100$$

1.2 Host range studies of rice root knot nematode in different varieties of rice crops

Some common ten varieties of rice viz; Dharam, Tampha, RCM-9, SK, Ayangleima, Jatra, Mamingthondabi, Thangjing, Priya and Lamyanba were subjected to screening for resistance against root knot nematode *Meloidogyne graminicola* during July to November 2012 in 2 kg capacity tub. Germinated seeds of each variety were sown in tubs (15 cm height, 50 cm diameter) filled with steam sterilized soil at the rate of 10 seeds per tub. When the seedlings were 15 days old, the seedlings were inoculated with 5000 second stage juveniles of *Meloidogyne graminicola* in three replicates. Three months after inoculation plants were uprooted, washed, cleaned and then fixed in 4% formaline. Staining was done in lactophenol aniline blue and cleared in pure lactophenol and observation were made on the number of galls, number of seeds, plant height, fresh anddry weight of root and shoot and final nematode population of the soil for each tub. Root gall index was assessed on 0-5 scale.

RESULTS AND DISCUSSION

1.1 Survey on incidence of rice root knot nematode on different rice fields of Manipur

The incidence of rice root knot nematode *M. graminicola* of intensity of infection, root knot index and number of galls of four plain districts namely Imphal east, Imphal west Thoubal and Bishenpur district of Manipur are given in Table 1.1a, b, c and d,. In this survey altogether 41 localities were foud infested with rice root knot nematode. but there were varying of their disease incid ence. Some of plants were seriously infected with these pest but some have low disease infestation rate. Field survey revealed that *M. graminicola* was widely distributed in most rice growing areas of four plain districts of Manipur. Rice root knot disease was more prevalent in dry bed condition than wet bed condition. Most of the farmers grew seedlings in upland (dry) soiland there was more rice root knot disease and second stage juvenile population in both nursery and seedling root. The galled (diseased) seedling had significantly shorter roots and shoots. Most of the farmers did not know about the nematode problem and did not follow any management practices to control it in nurseries and in the main field. This indicated high risk of multiplication of the nematodes and huge lost in rice production. Altogether seven plant parasitic nematode genera viz. *M. graminicola, Helicotylenchus multicintus, Tylenchorhynchus sp, Pratylenchus sp, Hoplolaimus sp, Xiphinema sp,* and *Criconematodes sp,* were found associated with different varieties of rice during this investigation.

Although several plant parasitic nematodes are encounterd with rice root knot nematode but frequently encountered genera of six types was only selected. The highest number of *M. graminicola* (12423) was recorded in chabokpi variety of rice at Checkon loukon of paurabi followed by Kanglou loukon (6614) of Imphal East. Next to it is the Maniyaiskul loukon (3400) of Imphal East, Malom loukol (3060) of Imphal west, Checkon loukon (2423) of Imphal East, Bishenpur mamang loukon (2045) of Bisnupur District, Irengbam loukon (1800) of Bisnupur, Kheckman loukol (1345) of Thoubal District, Dolaithabi loukol (1175) of Thoubal District, Serou loukol (1020) of Thoubal District, Mekola loukol (1010) of Imphal west district, Yaral loukol (950) of Imphal west district, Kakmayai loukol (560) of Thoubal district, Maibam lokpa ching (408) of Imphal west, Maibam loukol (150) of Bisnupur District, Kharou loukol (135) of Imphal East, Bamon loukol (120) of Imphal east, Utlou loukol (102) of Imphal west.

According to Sasser (1979) root knot nematode *M. graminicola* was remarked as potential factor for damaging rice crops in the tropics. The present investigation also supports the work of Das and Das (2000), who reported about the prevalence of *Meloidogyne* species on vegetable crops in Assam and Arunachal Pradesh. The work also agree with the investigation of Khan et. al. (2000) on recent studies of prevalence root knot nematode *Meloydogyne* spp. in twenty plain and ten hilly district of Uttar Pradesh. There preferences were highest with brinjal followed by cucumber, okra, tomato, pepper and lowest with cabbage and cauliflower.

The results supported the works of Sharma et.al.2002 about the population and effect of rice root knot nematode in diseased and healthy looking rice plants and their distribution in rice field. Pokharel (2009) also reported about the damage of root knot nematode *M. graminicola* to rice in fields with different soil types. The present investigation also agree about the works of Rao and Biswas (1973) on evaluation of field losses in rice due to the root knot nematode. The reports supported works of Babotola (1984) who investigated on rice nematode problem in Nigeria, their occurrence, distribution and pathogenecity on rice. Villanueva et.al. (1992) also reported on occurrence of plant parasitic nematodes associated with upland rice in the Phillipes. Coyne et.al (1999) worked out on prevalence of plant parasitic nematodes associated with rice in Ghana, the present investigation agree with the reports of their findings. The reports of present findings are in adjustable conformity with the works of Prasad et.al (1985) about the occurrence of the root knot nematodes *M. graminicola* in semi deep water rice.

The root knot nematodes inhabit in areas with average annual temperatures between 15⁰ C and 33⁰ C (Sasser and Carter, 1985). The temperature of Manipur falls between this suitable range which makes the root knot nematode survive successfully. Among vegetables tomato suffered comparatively more than brinjal and other crops (Jain et al, 2007). Chandel *et al.* (2002) studied the population behavior of root-knot nematode, *Meloidogyne triticoryzae* in the five rice based cropping systems viz., rice-wheat, rice-wheatgreengram, rice berseem, rice-potato-greengram and rice-mustard-greengram for a period of two years. The results revealed that the peak population density occurred in September in the rice crop. The other crops in the Rabi and summer seasons had a profound influence on the height of the peak in the succeeding rice crop. Some level of reproduction occurred in wheat, greengram and berseem in Rabi which contributed to relatively higher equilibrium densities. The potato variety Pusa Bahar increased the population density while Pusa Badshah decreased it. The lower temperature during the Rabi season also limited the rate of population growth. Chandel et al., (2002) studied the effect of puddling and water regimes on hydraulic conductivity (cm/day) of soil, bulk density (mg/m3) and population density of rice root-knot nematode, Meloidogyne triticoryzae in experimental rice field. They reported that population density of M. triticoryzae declined in puddled soil. The invasion of the roots by the second generation infective juveniles was reduced. Population density was higher in the non-puddled soil, especially in unsubmerged condition compared to puddled and submerged soil Thus in association with root knot nematode *Meloidogyne sp.* other important plant parasitic nematodes are also fond in the infested soil which co-ordinately infect the host. Reddy et.al. (1972) also worked out existence of root knot nematode *M. incognita* with other plant parasitic nematodes. Like the present findings, Ali (1989) also reported 15 genera of plant parasitic nematodes in association with *Meloidogyne* spp. And *Helicotylenchus* spp. were found as dominated groups. The finding support the view of Reddy and Singh (1979) who worked out *Tylenchulus* spp., *Pratylenchus* spp., *Hoplolaimus* spp. And *Meloidogyne* spp. as pathogenic factor infecting citrus root. Sharma (1987) also reported *Meloidogyne* spp. As important encountered genera along with other parasitic nematodes infecting many pulse crops. Rautaray et. al. (1987) worked out nemic association of plant parasitic nematodes with *M. incognita* infested ginger and turmeric in Orissa and *M. incognita* was found commonly encountered nematode next to *Macroposthonia ornato* infecting ginger. The results are in adjustable conformity with the works of Devrajan, 2001, who reported on the association of plant parasitic nematodes with cultivated crops of Tamirabarani river basin in Tamil Nadu. Among the nematodes observed, *Helicotylenchus multicinctus, Pratylenchus coffeae, Radopholus similes, Meloidogyne incognita, Hoplolaimus* spp. And *H. multicinctus* occurred more frequently. Khan and Ahmad (2000) conducted a survey in Punjab Province of Pakistan and revealed hat out of 1217 samples collected, 498 samples were found to be infested with root-knot nematodes. They observed that *M. incognita* was widely distributed species followed by *M. javanica*. Anamika *et al.* (2011) conducted a survey in 21 districts of Uttar Pradesh on crops of rice, tomato, okra, cowpea, onion, pumpkin, brinjal and bitter gourd to assess the incidence and intensity of root-knot disease. Attacked plants showed heavy galling, root decay or reduced root system, yellowish foliage, unthrifty growth and small slow growing fruits and poor yields. Khan and Anwer (2011) conducted surveys in Aligarh and Hathras districts of Uttar Pradesh and observed that the *Meloidogyne graminicola* was found widely distributed in most of the rice growing localities. Khan *et al.* (2011) recorded the occurrence of seven 30 plant parasitic nematode species associated with some important crops and two weeds in Andaman and Nicobar Islands, India. Many other works have also documented association of plant parasitic nematodes with various crops in India and include –Senthil kumar and Rajendran (2005) in Tamilnadu; Joymati and Mema (2007) in Manipur and Tiwari *et al.*, (2000) and Rathour *et al.*, (2010) in Madhya Pradesh. Community analysis of plant parasitic nematodes have been studied by Ansari and Ahmed (2000) in Guava, and Srinivasan *et al.*, (2011) in banana, Thanjavoor, Tamilnadu. Khan *et al.*, (2010) reported nematode diseases in various crop plants of Chhattisgarh including -*Aphelenchoides besseyii* in Rice, *R. reniformis* in Pulse crops, *Meloidogyne* spp. and *M. incognita* in Vegetable crops and *R. similis* in Banana Review of literature reveals that studies on plant nematodes in India are mostly restricted to states, such as, Gujarat, Karnataka, Orissa, Tamil nadu, Haryana, Madhya Pradesh, Assam, U.P, West Bengal, Himachal Pradesh, Rajasthan, Kerela, Andhra Pradesh and Punjab (Ali and Koshy, 1982; Khan and Khan, 1991; Muniyappa, , 2003; Naidu *et al.*, 2007; Prasad *et al.*, 2006; Rathore *et al.*, 2003 and Singh *et al.*, 1979), where ICAR centers exist. The only work yet documented on the nematode diseases of plants in Chhattisgarh state include Sao *et al.* (2008) and Sahu *et al.* (2011). Thus, a survey of nematode diseases of vegetable crops grown in this state becomes practically relevant. The root knot nematode was selected for the purpose. Community analysis of plant nematodes populations is also important, not only to assess the pathogenic potential of the nematodes in a particular region, but is also an important criteria for identification of hotspots of nematode attack. RecentlyRavindra et.al. (2013) reported occurrence of rice root knot nematode at Karnataka infecting onion. Ravichandra et.al. (2003) also reported occurrence and distribution of phytoparasitic nematodes associated with rice in Mandhya district Karnataka.

.

1.2 Host range studies of rice root knot nematode in different varieties of rice crops

Data presented I.3a table 1.3b indicated the pathogenicity of *Meloidogyne graminicola* on rice varieties viz: Dharam, Tampha, RCM-9, SK, Ayangleima, Jatra, Maminthondabi, Thangjing, Priya and Lamyanba. Rice variety Lamyanba showed maxnimum root length 10 cm, shoot length 45 cm, fresh shoot weight 22g, fresh root weight 3.4 g, number of seeds 100, number of galls 45 and total nematode population 11000, followed by rice variety Priya and Thangjing. Rice varity Dharum showed maximum root length 15 cm, shoot length 60 cm, fresh shoot weight 44 g, fresh root weight 5.3 g, number of seeds 375, which was followed by Tampha and RCM-9.

Out of the 10 varieties, Dharam was recorded as moderately resistant variety against root-knot nematode followed by rice variety Tampha were recorded. SRCM-9, SK, Ayangleima, Jatra were recorded as susceptible whereas Mamingthondabi, Thangjing, Priya, Lamyanba were recorded as highly susceptible.

The present investigation is in conformity with Gitanjali et.al. (2007) who screened 8 rice varieties, screening rice varieties for resistance against root knot nematode (*Meloidogyne graminicola).* Anil Prashar *et al.* (2004) clearly demonstrated that the severity of *Meloidogyne graminicola* to rice increases with increase of water stress, hence the important of using rice cultivars that are tolerant to water stress and resistant to the nematode. Kalita *et al.* (2004) screened twelve commonly cultivated rice cultivars against rice root knot nematode (*Meloidogyne graminicola*) in sick soil under greenhouse condition.

The resuls supports the findings of resistant varieties of Pea by Usuma and Aparajita (2013) against root knot nematode *Meloidogyne incognita*. Likewise not the same crop but similar works also reported by Neelam and Lukman khan (2013) for screening of resistant varieties of strawberry against root knot nematodes *Meloidogyne sp*. Chandradas et.al. (2011) also reported screening of banana hybrid for screening of resistant varieties against root knot nematodes *Meloidogyne incognita*.

Vinodkumar et.al. (2011) also investigated reaction of cowpea genotypes against Reniform nematode *Rotylenchulus reniformis*. Fazal Ahmad et.al. (2002) worked out screening of soybean varieties for their resistance against *M. incognita*. Daman Jeet Kaur (2005) worked out about the effect of rice root knot nematode *Meloidogyne graminicola* on wheat in rice wheat cropping system.

From the above investigation it can be suggest that resistance is one of several tools for use in an integrated approach for root knot nematode management. Two primary attributes of host resistance for nematode management are relevant a) the value of resistance infection and b) the rotational value of resistance in cropping systems for protecting subsequent crops, based on the ability to suppress nematode population densities in soil by restricting nematode reproduction. These two attributes underpin most nematode resistance breeding and management decisions. Resistant lines will be proved useful parents for root knot nematode resistant breeding programme.

Chapter - 2

Management Studies

2.1 Collection of different medicinal plants from different localities in plan districts of Manipur

The plant materials were collected from natural and cultivated habitates. Altogether ten medicinal plants were selected for these management studies of rice root knot nematode *Meloidogyne graminicola*. The selected plants are *Phlogacanthus thyrsiformis, Acorus calamus, Zanthoxylum acanthopodium. Parkia javanica, Vitex negundo, Tagetes patula, Melia azedarach, Plumeria rubra, Jatropha curcas and Ficus hispida* were collected from different localities of Manipur.

2.2 Preparation of different essential oil extracts from the collected medicinal plants

Healthy leaves of leaves of *Phlogacanthus thyrsiformis, Acorus calamus, Zanthoxylum acanthopodium. Parkia javanica, Vitex negundo, Tagetes patula, Melia azedarach, Plumeria rubra, Jatropha curcas and Ficus hispida* were collected from different localities of Manipur The plants were collected from their natural habitate, washed with water and oven dried at 58+2°C for 48 hrs before making into powder with the help of a domestic grinder. For extraction of oil 500g dry weight of each plant product was taken and dissolved in 500 ml of distilled water and the essential oil extraction was done with the help of Clevenger apparatus (Carvatho et.al. 1981). The solvent was distilled off and transferred into a separate beaker, which was completely evaporated from the extract in oven till it become a semi solid material. Triton X 100 was used as emulsifier of oil for experimental uses.

2.3 Management

Rice is the stable food of the country after wheat and largest cultivated area among all food grains in India. *Meloidogyne graminicola* is a serious pest of rice and causing extensive damage to rice crop in many countries of the world including India. For several decades the management of plant parasite nematodes has been mainly dominated by the use of synthetic chemical nematicides. But their application is problematic because of many negative environmental impacts and consequently many good nematicides have been withdrawn from the market. Therefore, there is a strong demand to develop more sustainable and environmentally benign method for nematodes control. Plant parasitic nematode is hidden enemies and continues to tearing farmers for successful and profitable cultivation of this agricultural crop. Root knot nematodes, *Meloidogyne* spp. are recognized as the most economically important genus of plant parasitic nematodes worldwide. They cause severe damage and high yield losses to a large no of cultivated plants especially on vegetable crop in the tropics, sub-tropics (Netscher & Sikora, 1990) & are most widespread tiny organisms which limits worlds agricultural productivity (Sasser et.al., 1982, Taylor et.al. 1982) They attack almost all the cultivated plants but vegetable crops are their most preferred host (Sasser, 1980). More than 600 known species of medicinal plants are grown in Manipur (**Sinha, 1996**). Although several important medicinal plants were grown in our state, but due to lack of knowledge about the nematicidal properties, not much work have developed for using them in nematode control practices. Further, it will open an alternative nematode control method or less toxic nematicides needs to be developed and the only way is the searching for such nematicidal compound is to screen naturally occurring compounds in plants. Thus, the present investigation has undertaken to evaluate the essential oil products obtain from 10 indigenous medicinal plants of Manipur viz. leaves of *Phlogacanthus thyrsiformis, Acorus calamus,*

Zanthoxylum acanthopodium. Parkia javanica, Vitex negundo, Tagetes patula, Melia azedarach, Plumeria rubra, Jatropha curcas and Ficus hispida were collected from different localities of Manipur.

The root knot nematode *Meloidogyne sp.* cause enormous losses to many economically important crops throughout the world **(Webster, 1972)** and is one of the major limiting factor affecting the production of vegetables in India **(Reddy, 1988).** It causes severe damage and yield losses to a wide group of cultivated plants especially on vegetable crops in all parts of India **(Khan and khan, 1996).** Once the plant is infected by this nematode treatment options are very limited. Use of chemical nematicides create environmental problems and they are very expensive. This leads to the development of alternate strategies in the nematode management. One of the promising alternative is the use of the plant products to observed the possibility of their nematicidal/ nematostatic properties for the management of the nematode problem. Though most of the researcher have investigated leaves, root and valuable constituents of the plants for nematicidal activities. **(Siddiqui et.al. 1987; Prakash & Rao, 1997; Muhammad et.al. 2001).** Thus, the present status about management of root knot nematode control is highly essential and the following investigation has taken up as details below:

2.3. (a) Laboratory Condition

Efficacy of essential oil extracts obtained from the selected 10 medicinal plants against egg hatching and larval mortality of *M. graminicola.*

b) **Pot Experiment**

   Efficacy of essential oil extracts of medicinal plants gainst rice root knot nematode *Meloidogyne graminicala* in pots.

c) **Evaluation of essential oils of medicinal plants against rice root knot pest in Manipur**

d) **One day training program for transfer of technology to the farmers.**

REVIEW LITERATURE

Rice is believed to have first been domesticated in India, although the oldest surviving written record telling of its existence 500 years ago is from China. It is staple food for about half of the population of our planet and 80% or more of the world rice production is reported to be cultivated in the highly populated southern and eastern parts of Asia. Rice is grown in almost all the states of India as a principal food crop. Root knot nematode, *Meloidogyne graminicola* is recognized as one of the serious nematode pest of rice that causes root knot diseases characterised by the presence of root galls or knot on the roots, yellowing, stunting and wilting of the plant is related to nematode-to-root biomass ratio (Singh *et al*, 2006). Nationally, *M. graminicola* is reported to cause upto 50% loss in grain yield (Rao & Biswas, 1973) and in severe cases it may go upto 64% (Phukan. 1995) Losses in grain yield were also estimated to range from 16-32 % due to this nematode (Rao & Biswas, 1973). This diseases is widely distributed in rice growing areas of the world. Occurrence of the diseases was reported from different states of India by several workers including Western and Central part of Uttar Pradesh (Kamalwanshi *et al*, 2002 and Pankaj *et al*, 2010

Root knot nematodes, *Meloidogyne* spp. represent an economically important group of parasitic phytonematodes. They are distributed worldwide and parasitize monocotyledons, decotyledons, herbaceous & woody plants (Eisenback and Hirschmann, 1979). In economic terms they cause an estimated loss of about $ 157 billion annually to world agriculture (Abad et.al. 2008) & in case of India Agriculture is estimated at about Rs. 210 crore annually (Jain et.al. 2007).

Oyedunmade (1996) from Nigeria reported that used of ash powder of neem, parkia and crotolaria leaves when applied as soil amendment against root knot nematode *M. incognita* infecting cowpea shows reduction of disease incidence and improvement in overall plant growth parameters Yuji et.al. (2000) worked out nematicidal activity of essential oils extracted from 27 species including aromatic plants and twelve of the 27 essential oils immobilized more than 80% of juvenile of *M. javanica* and their results suggest that essential oils and their main components may serve as nematicides. Essential oils of some plants and their components have been tested for nematicidal activity in vitro and in soil (Oka et.al. 2000, Alvarez Castellanos et.al. 2001) Chitwood (2002) investigated about the presence of nematicidal compounds which have been isolated from species in the family Asteraceae. Perez et.al. (2003) reported that the essential oils of *Chrysanthemum coronarium* flowerheads showed strong nematicidal activity in vitro and in growth chamber experiments. Leaf extracts of *Crotolaria virgulata* sub sp. Grantia had a nemostatic effect on the J2 of *M. incognita* at the same low concentration (Jourand et.al. 2003) Ibrahim et.al (2006) investigated about the essential oil and plant extracts on hatching migration and mortality of root knot nematode and found that essential oils from their plants shows promising sources for nematicides.

Use of essential oils obtained from locally growing plants for nematode control practices has been tried out by different workers Lella et.al. (1992) and Gokte et.al. (1991). Chandra vardana et.al. (1996) reported about the essential oil extracts obtained from 21 different medicinal plants in terms of larval mortality and found effective. Saravanapriya et.al. (2004) also investigated seed extract of *Areaca catechee*, left extracts of *Tagetes erecta*, *A indica* and *Calotropis gigantic* causes significant inhibition of egg hatching even at lower concentration of 0.1%.

Elimination of an established root knot disease by chemicals is costly and sometimes hazardous. As an alternative to the chemical nematicides in recent times plant products are gaining importance in the management of root knot nematode. It is practicable, cheapest and effective method. The problem of pesticide resistance to control the environmental degradation and harmful effects associated with the use of synthetic broad spectrum pesticides have triggered the interest of scientist in exploring alternate pest control measures. The main objective for management studies is to improve plant growth and to increase the yield product. It is a great challenge to new research efforts for evolving nematode management practices which are economical and ecofriendly. The use of plant and plant products having nematicidal properties involved low cost which are easy to apply and produce no pollution hazards.

Since the time immemorial our traditional system of medicine and folklore claiming that medicinal plants as whole or their parts are being used in all types of disease successfully including anti bacterial, antihelminthic and anti-inflammatory etc. The plant kingdom has long been sources of medicines and continues to contribute significantly to the development of today's pharmaceuticals (cragg et.al. 1977). Traditionally used medicinal plants have recently attracted the attention of the biological scientific communities. This has been involved the isolation and the identification of the secondary metabolities produced by the plants and their use as active principles in medicinal preparations (Taylor et.al. 2001). Currently, most medications including antibiotics, anticancer drugs and drugs directed against parasites are based on natural compounds (Wink, 2008; Wink et.al. 2007, Schafer and Wink, 2009). Important subclass of secondary metabolities in natural products includes phenol, phenolic acids, quinines, flavones, flavonids, flavonols, tannins etc.

The survey of literature indicates that studies related isolation and characterization of secondary metabolites of nematicidal effect are scarce in India particularly in North Eastern States of India. In view of the fact that there have been nonexistent of data, the present study was proposed to undertaken. Medicinal plants traditionally have been used to treat diseases in India, since at least 3500-1800, BC according to the evidences in the Rig-Veda. Using plants as principal sources of medicine inherent in traditional Indian medicine. In fact many currently available drugs were derived from such plants (Singh, 2001) Ayurveda and other Indian systems use plants or plants products to treat various ailments. Of 45000 plant species in India, 3000 plants are officially documented for their medicinal properties. However about 6000 plants processing medicinal properties including antibacterial and antiprotozoal activity are said to be used by traditional practitioners.

Whether for traditional use- validation or drug discovery purpose, previous studies have focussed on the antibacterial potential of medicinal plants (Subramnium, 1999). Investigation was restricted to whether or not a plant could kill or inhibit the growth of the bacteria. However this is only one facet of a plants anti-infective potential. The antipathogenic properties of plants have received much less attention, but may be just as important in combating disease as their antibacterial counterparts. The interruption of the quorum sensing (QS) or bacterial cell to cell communication is one example of the antipathogenic effect. Since a large number of systems affecting pathogenecity are controlled by QS, interrupting this communication system can render pathogenic bacteria non-virulent (Zhang and Patel 2004). Patel *et al* in 2010, reported that the ethanol extracts of whole plant materials of *Eupatorium odoratum* showed significant antihelminthic activity.

Recently in Manipur, only preliminary works for management of root knot nematode using essential oils extracts was started by Joymati & Dhanachand (2000) infecting soyabean and found significant reduction in disease infestation and overall improvement of plant growth parameters. In continuation of the root knot management practices, several works in different methodology was done using medicinal plant products as bio control agents by Joymati (2005, 2006, 2007, 2008, 2009 & 2010, 2011, 2012, 2013) and found effective. Thus, the proposed research programme was taken up to cope up the gap knowledge of nematicidal properties present in the medicinal plants of Manipur.

MATERIALS AND METHOD

2.3 (a) Laboratory Condition

Efficacy of essential oil extracts obtained from the selected 10 medicinal plants against egg hatching and larval mortality of *M. graminicola.*

Plant extract preparation.

Healthy leaves of *V. negunda, J. curcas, P. acutifolia, Ph. thyrsiflorus, M. azedarach, Z. acanthopodium, T. patula, F. hispida, P. javanica and*

A. calamus were collected. The collected leaves were washed with water & dried in shade. The dried materials were made into powder with the help of a clean grinder. 20 gm (dry weight) of each plant product were taken and distillation of essential oil was done with the help of Clevenger apparatus. The solvent was distilled off and the content was transferred to a separate beaker. The solvent was evaporated from the extract in oven till it become a semisolid material. A Stock solution of 1000ppm was prepared in distilled water with 1 percent Triton x-100 as emulsifier & from it further dilution such as 1, 10, 100, and 1000ppm were prepared by adding required amount of distilled water.

Effect on egg hatching

Sodium hypochlorite was utilized for isolation of nematode eggs from root galls according to Hussey and Barker (1973). One hundred eggs were transferred to a cavity block containing 5ml of oil extracts of different concentrations. Eggs in distilled water were treated as control. All treatments were replicated three times. Mean egg hatching was counted at an intervals of 12, 24 & 48 hr after treatment.

In a similar experiment set up hatched second stage juveniles of *M. gramnicola* were transferred into the cavity block (100juveniles|cavityblock) containing different concentrations of oils extracts (5ml|cavity block) Juveniles put in distilled water were treated as control. There were three replications for each treatment. Juveniles mortality rate was counted at intervals of 12, 24 and 48 h after treatment. Those larvae which did not response to the touch by a fine needle were counted as dead.

2.3 (b) Pot Experiment

Efficacy of essential oil extracts of medicinal plants gainst rice root knot nematode *Meloidogyne graminicala* in pots

Healthy leaves of *Parkia javanica, Zanthoxylum acanthopodium, Jatropha curcas, Vitex negundo* and *Adatoda vasica* were collected, washed with water and oven dried at 58±2°C for 48 hours before making into powder with the help of a domestic grinder. For extraction of oil 50g dry weight of each plant porduct was taken and the essential oil extracts was done with the help of Clevenger apparatus. The solvent was distilled off and transferred into a separate beaker, which was completely evaporated from the extract in oven till it become semi solid material. The essential oil extracts was emulsified with triton X-100 as emulsifier. The seeds of rice plant (Dharam local variety) were soaked in stock solution of different oil extract mention above for 24 hours. Then, the seeds were spread and allow to dry under shade condition before sowing. The seeds were soaked in distilled water served as control. The seed from each treatment were sown in 30 cm tub containing 5 kg soil. Each treatment were replicated three times. After three weeks of sowing, plants were inoculated with freshly hatched 1000 J2 of *Meloidogyne graminicola*. The control was also inoculated and replicated three times.

Thirty five days after inoculation of J2 the mature plants were uprooted with the help of hoe and gently washed with running tap water.
The plants were cut at the margin of root and shoot. Length of the root and the shoot was measured with the help of meter scale. Fresh weight of the root and the shoot was determined by physical balance. Root and shoot were kept separately in paper envelopes and kept in an incubator maintained at 58 ° C for 5 days. Dry weight of root and shoot was determined. The number of grains were also counted. Number of galls, root knot index (0-5 scale) and final nematode population (both in soil and root) were also recorded.

2.3 (c) Evaluation of essential oils of medicinal plants against rice root knot pest in Manipur

Healthy leaves of *Tagetes patula, Ficus hispida, Acrorus calamus, Plumeria acutifolia* & *Melia azedarach* were collected, washed with water and oven dried at 58^{+} ° C for 48 hours before making into powder with the help of a domestic grinder. For extraction of oil 50 gm dry weight of each plant product was taken and the essential oil extracts was done with the help of Clevenger apparatus. The solvent was distilled off and transferred into a separate beaker, which was completely evaporated from the extract in oven till it become semi solid material. The essential oil extracts was emulsified with triton X-100 as emulsifier.

The seeds of rice plant (Tampha local variety) were soaked in stock solution of 100ppm concentration for 24 hours. Then the seeds were spread and allow to dry under shade condition before sowing. The seeds soaked in distilled water served as control. The seed from each treatment were sown in 30 cm tub containing 5kg autoclaved soil. Each treatment were replicated three times. After three week of sowing, plants were inoculated with freshly hatched J2 of *M. graminicola*, one Juvenile/gm of soil. The control was also inoculated and replicated three times.

Thirty five days after inoculation of J2 the mature plants were uprooted with the help of hoe & gently washed with running tap water. The plants were cut at the margin of root and shoot. Length of the root and the shoot was measured with the help of meter scale. Fresh weight of the root and the shoot was determined by physical balance. Root and shoot were kept separately in paper envelopes and kept in an incubator maintained at 58°C for 5 days. Dry weight of root and shoot was determined. The number of grains were also counted. Number of galls, root knot index (0-5 scale) and final nematode population (both in soil & root) were also recorded.

RESULTS AND DISCUSSION

2.3 (a) Laboratory Condition

Efficacy of essential oil extracts obtained from the selected 10 medicinal plants against egg hatching and larval mortality of *M. graminicola*

Effect of essential oil extracts obtained from 10 different medicinal plants on eggs of *M. graminicola* was shown in Table 2.3ai. Egg hatching was maximum in control although among treated one highest hatching rate was observed in 1ppm concentration at 48 hrs in all plant extracts.

Among these 10 medicinal plants oil extracts obtained from *Tagetes patula* showed most inhibitory effect followed by extracts of *Jatropha curcas*. Essential oil obtained from Ficus hispida found least effective among tested plants. The rate of hatching was directly proportional with exposure period and inversely proportional with concentration of extract as it was decreased with increase in extract concentration as highest rate observed in 1ppm and lowest rate at 1000ppm concentration in all oil extracts tested.

The essential oil Extracts obtained from *T. patula* observed most nematicidal activity which showed cent percent larval mortality within 12 hrs in 1000ppm concentration followed by extracts of Jatropha cuscas at rate of mortality was directly proportional with exposure period& concentration of extracts being maximum at 48hrs in 1000ppm concentration in all oil extracts of tested plants as shown in Table 2.3aii. Among this 10selected plants *T. patula* oil extracts shows most inhibitory effect & extracts of F. hispida was least effective on Juvenile mortality as well as on egg hatching.

The above investigation supported works of Yuji Oka et.al. (2000) who reported about the activity of some essential oils extracted from 27 species and aromatic plants in vitro and in pots. It was found that essential oil of *Carum carvi, Foeniculum valgare, Mentha rotundifolia, Mentha spicata, Orignum valgare, O. syriacum and Coridothymus capitatus* have some nematicidal potential against root knot nematodes. The result agree with the works of Olabiyi (2008) reported that aqueous extracts from the roots of marigold, nitha and basil plant reduced root knot nematode population in the soil with corresponding increases in plant height plant leaf and fruit yield. The findings agree with the works of Khan et.al. (2008) who examined the effect of ethanol extracts of *Azadirachta indica, Withania somnifera, Tagetes ercta and Eucalyptus citriodora* against nematode associated with papaya. The experiment showed reduction in gall index, the number of juveniles and egg masses in all the treatments. The present investigation provides valuable data on medicinal plants provide a wide support for nematicidal activity &

can be used as possible bases in agriculture as pesticide. Inclusion of plant botanicals into soils alone or with bio control agents has been recommended as a substitute safe & effective control method for management of plant parasitic nematodes. There is need for further work to elucidate the specific active substances for onward transfer to peasant farmers to manage nematode on there are able lands to increase crop yield. Natural plant products have the ability to produce environmentally friendly bio-toxicants that are biodegradable and efficacious against pathogenic organisms including soil inhabiting plant parasitic nematodes (Schmutter, 1990, Jackai et.al. 1992).

Plant Parasitic nematodes are the main pathogens on most fiber crops, horticultural, food and vegetable crops and without adequate control cause loss of yield and quality. Approximate yield losses due to plant parasitic nematodes have been estimated to be $100 billion worldwide each year (sasser and Freckman, 1987). Root–knot nematodes (*Meloidogyne* species) infect almost all types of plants and may cause considerable damage (Adekunle and Akinlua, 2007). Root knot nematodes larvae infect plant causing the development of root knot galls that drains the plants photosynthetic and nutrient (Esenback & Triantaphyllous, 1990). These nematodes may be controlled by cultural practices, chemical nematicides and the use of resistant cultivars. Although chemical nematicides hold major promise in the nematode control system but the high costs, non availability at the time of need and the hazards they pose as environmental pollutants discourage most potential user (Elabadri et.al. 2008).

The investigation are in conformity with the works of **Joymati et al** (1998) who investigated different plant parts of ***L. camera, J. curcas, M. purpusilla, J. multiflorum*** and ***M. pudica*** against eggs and second stage juveniles of ***M. incognita*** and among these plant aqueous extracts obtained from ***M. purpusilla*** and ***J. multiflorum*** were found more inhibitory effect and among plant parts seed and flower extracts was most inhibitory followed by leave and stem extracts. The nematicidal activitics of aqueous extracts of different parts of ***Tagetes erecta*** on egg masses, larval mortality and invasion of larvae to Brinjal has been reported by **Dhanger et al (1996).** The results are in similar conformity with the work of **Pandey (1990).** The concern plants were ***A. majus, A. annua, A. pallens and L. sativa*** against egg hatching and juvenile mortality. Highest mortality rate was found in 'S' dilution of ***A. majus*** and highest inhibition in complete hatching of juveniles also found with this same plant extracts with same concentrations.

The present investigations are in adjustable conformity with the finding of **Chandravadana et. al. (1996)** who tested with 21 extracts obtain from 12 edible plants species viz. methanol extracts of root and seeds of ***B. oleracea L., C. morifolium L., G. superb, S. viarum*** etc. against ***M. incognita*** juveniles for their larval mortality. They observed that the methanol extracts of periwinkle roots and defatted onion (***A. cepa***) seeds and the essential oil of scented geranium (***P. graveolens***) shows significant nematicidal activity against ***M. incognita.*** The methanol extracts of the seeds of Malabar glory lily (***G. superb***) also showed moderate activity. The work also supported the findings of **Nidiry et al (1994)** who investigated seed extracts of ***G. superb*** against ***M. incognita*** juvenile for their larval mortality and found inhibitory effect. Likewise the present report **Lella et al (1992)** work out essential oil extracts of ***P. graviolens*** against root knot nematode and found nematicidal effect. **Chandravadana et al (1994)** reported effect of serpentine oil against ***M. incognita*** juveniles and found inhibitory effect which agrees with the present findings.

2.3 (b) Pot Experiment

Efficacy of essential oil extracts of medicinal plants gainst rice root knot nematode *Meloidogyne graminicola* in pots

The germination percentage of rice seeds was not affected by seed treatment with oil extract of medicinal plant and it was similar and better in all the treatments (Table 2.3.b.i). In general, all the treatment showed better plant growth but also reduced the damage by root knot infestation of rice as compared to control. It is clearly indicated from the data in Table 2.3.b.i that shoot and root length of rice plant treated with *Jatropha curcas* was maximum followed by rice plant treated with *Adhotoda vasica*. The highest number of grains was also recorded in *Jatropha curcas* treated plant. The essential oil extract of *Zanthoxylum acanthopodium* was found to be least effective among the plant extracts.

In case of the incidence of diseases, there were reduction in infestation rate in *Jatropha curcas* oil extract treated plant by recording 7 galls and total polulation of only 580 indicating nearly half times reduction from initial inoculum level whereas in case of untreated one 23 number of galls with1690 nematode population were recorded indicating one and half times increased in population level (Table 2.3.b.ii). The results supported works of Stirpe et.al. 1976 who reported that *Jatropha* oil cake is toxic to mammals due to presence of curcin and alectin which is conformity with the present findings. The seed oil of *Jatropha* is also reported to possess insecticidal, mollucicidal, fungicidal and nematicidal properties (Chitra and Dhyani, 2006). Similar results was obtained on reduction of root knot galls and total population with the use of botanicals as reported by Verma and Khan (2004). Plant treated with the oil extract of *Zanthopodium acanthopodium* was found to be least effective with the 16 number galls and 1310 nematode population. From the above observations, it can be concluded that treated plants had low infestation rate and improvement in overall growth parameters in comparison to control but inoculated one (Table 2.3.b.i and 2.3.b.ii.).

The present investigation is in conformity with those reported by Kumar *et al.* (2011) they also reported management of root knot and reniform nematode in pots and suggested the effectiveness of the oil extracts of sacred basil over the other extracts. This study was supported by Bora and Neog (2006) who tested oil cakes against root knot nematode larvae in terms of their mortality rate. The work also supported the finding of Haider and Askary (2011) investigated seed extracts of 17 plant extracts against *M. incognita* juvenile for their larval mortality and found inhibitory effects. Hena *et al.* (2009) tried out different extracts of plants against *M. incognita* and found effective. The above investigation supported works of Joymati et. al 2012 who reported the essential oil extract of medicinal plants was found to be effective against the root knot nematode on kidney bean. Prasad *et al.* (2002) reported some plant extracts were toxic to root knot nematode and further application in pots enhanced plant growth signjficantly with reduction in the nematode population

According to Chopra et al (1956) all the test plants contain alkaloid principles and several compounds which act as inhibitory substances to the nematodes. Bitter glucid in ***T. grandis***, plumeric acid in ***A. vesica*** salycyclic acid in ***J. multiflorum***, bitter resin, saccharine and margosine in ***M. azedarach***, nyctanthin and alkaloid in ***P. javanica***, bitter principal in ***C. indicum*** and tanic acid in ***A. paniculata***.

The present investigation is in an adjustable conformity with the results of Gokte et al (1991) who reported seven different oil extracts against root knot and cyst nematode and expressed their view in oil extracts of Indian basil and sacred basil to be most effective among other extracts.

These results are in agreement with Ononuju & Okoye (2003) with ***Azadirachta indica, Pennisetum purpureum, Imperata cylindrical, Ananas comosus*** and ***Cynodon dactylon***. Ononuju & Kalu (2004) made similar observations with ***Vernonia armygdaina and Rauwolfia vomitoria on Meloidogyne*** spp. Joymati (2009) also reported about the effect of chloroform methanol abstracts of different medicinal plants on egg hatching and larval mortality of ***M. incognita*** which support this result.

The significant increase in the plant growth parameters and seed weight recorded in treated plants when compare with untreated one, could be attributed in the reduction of root knot infestation by the essential oil extracts of the test plant.

2.3 (c) Evaluation of essential oils of medicinal plants against rice root knot pest in Manipur

The germination percentage of rice seeds was not affected by seed treatment with oil extract of medicinal plant and it was similar and better in all the treatments (Table 2.3.c.i). In general, all the treatment showed better plant growth but also reduced the damage by root knot infestation of rice as compound to control. It is clearly indicated from the data in Table 2.3.c.i that shoot and root length of rice plant treated with *Tagetes patula* was maximum followed by the rice plant treated with *Acrorus calamus*. The highest number of grains was also recorded in *Tagetes patula* treated plant. The essential oil extract of *Ficus hispida* was found to be least effective among the plant extracts.

In case of the incidence of diseases, there were reduction in infestation rate *in Tagetes patula* oil extract treated plant by recording 6 galls and total population of only 530 indicating nearly half times reduction from initial inoculums level whereas in case of untreated one 25 nos. of galls with 1760 nematode population were recorded indicating one and half times increased in population level (Table 2.3.c.ii). The work supported by the fundings of (Khan et. al. 2012b) who reported *Tagetes* spp. possess repelant and antagonistic character to several pathogens, especially nematode. Some important nematoxie compounds such as a tertheinyl have been found in *Tagetes* spp (Meijneke & Oostenbrink, 1957) which cause toxic effect on root knot nematode (Devakumar 1994).

The work is in adjustable conformity with the recent findings of Buena et al (root), who screened *T. patula* against some population of *M. incognita, M. javanice, M. arenaria* & *M. hapla* and concluded that marigold was resistant to all population except race of *M. hapla*. The report also supported the works of Supratoyo (1993) who studied on the effect of *Tagetes erecta* & *T. patula* for controlling plant parasitic rate on Banana.

The above investigation supported the work of Joymati (2009) who reported the essential oil extract of some medicinal plants against egg hatching and larval mentality & found *Andrographis panniculata* petroleum ether extracts was found most effective among tested oil extracts. The present investigation are in adjustable conformity with the findings of Chandravadana et al (1996) who tested twenty one oil extract obtained from 12 edible plants species against root knot nematode larva in term of their mortality rate and found effective.

Thus from the above findings it can be concluded that the investigation provide valuable data on medicinal plants provide a wide support for nematicidal activity and can be used as a possible basis in agriculture as pesticide. Inclussion of plant botanicals into soil alone or incorporation of plant product such as oil of preselected plants could provide a substitute, safe and effective control method for management of plant parasitic nematodes, *M. graminocola*. Thus, their is need for further work to elucidate the specific active substances for onward transfer to peasant farmers to manage nematodes on their arable land to increase crop yield. Lella et. al. (1992) also reported essential oil extracts of *P. graviolens* against root knot nematode and found nematicidal effect like the present findings. The results also agree with the investigations of Joymati and Dhanachand (2000) on the effect of essential oil extracts of some medicinal plants against root knot nematode on Soyabean. The findings supported the works of Joymati (2007) on evaluation of petroleum ether extracts of six different indigenous plants of Manipur against *M. incognita* in terms of larval mortality and egg hatching. It is therefore evident from the present study that the incorporation of such plant products can minimize the root knot nematode infestation.

According to Chopra et al (1956) all the test plants contain alkaloid principles and several compounds which act as inhibitory substances to the nematodes. Bitter glucid in ***T. grandis***, plumeric acid in ***M. globra*** salycyclic acid in ***X. longifolia***, bitter resin, saccharine and margosine in ***M. azedarach***, nyctanthin and alkaloid in ***O. sanctum.***

These results are in agreement with Ononuju & Okoye (2003) with ***Tectona grandis, Mussendra globra, Xylosoma longifolia, Ocimum sanctum and Melia azedarach***. Ononuju & Kalu (2004) made similar observations with ***Vernonia armygdaina and Rauwolfia vomitoria on Meloidogyne*** spp. The significant increase in the plant growth parameters and seed weight recorded in treated plants when compare with untreated one, could be attributed in the reduction of root knot infestation by the essential oil extracts of the test plant.

It is therefore concluded that the incorporation of plant products such as oils of pre selected plants could provide a suitable and cheaper alternative for management of root knot nematode *M. graminicola* which infesting rice crops.

Chemical Composition

CHEMICAL COMPOSITION of the 10 selected medicinal plants

Sl No.	Scientific Name	Local Name	Chemical Constituents	Medicinal uses
1.	***Tagetes patula***	French marigold (Haosanarei)	Presence of 25 isoquinoline alkaloids. Oxosarcocapnidine and oxocularin were present. The main components were piperitone (24.74%), piperitenone (22.93%), Terpinolene (7.8%) dihydrotagetone (4.91%), cis-tagetone (4.62%), limonene (4.52%) and allo-ocimene (3.66%).	Roots and seeds are purgative. essential oil from fresh heads is used as an antiseptic, as a fly repellant. Decoction of heads is used as carminative; juice contains iodine and applied to cuts and wound.
2.	***Vitex negundo***	Chaste tree (uriksibi)	Leaves: δ-guaiene, carryophyllene epoxide and ethyl-hexadecenoate. Flowers-δ-selinene, germacren-4-ol, carryophyllene epoxide and (E) -nerolidol. Fruit: β-selinene, α-cedrene, germacrene D and hexadecanoic acid.	Leaves, roots and fruits are used as medicine or tonic; expectorant, febrifuge and used in catarrh, fevers, foetid ulsers, rheumatism and gonorrhoea. Leaves and roots possess tranquilizing effect. Extract of leaves showed anticancer activity against Ehrlich ascites tumour cells. Leaves and roots are anthelmintic and used in dysentery and piles. Flowers are astringent, used in diarrhoea, fevers and liver complaints.

Sl No.	Scientific Name	Local Name	Chemical Constituents	Medicinal uses
3.	***Plumeria rubra***	Temple tree (Khagi leihao angangba)	Plumieride, Scopoletin, iridoides and volatile oils. All parts of Plumeria rubra contains iridoids: plumieride, the barks contain iridoids: fulvoplumierin, the root contains iridoids: 13-0-caffeoylplumieride, 13-deoxyplumieride, β-dihydroplumericinic acid, glucosyl ester plumenoside, 1α-plumieride, 8-isoplumieride, 1α-protoplumericin. Leaves contain bornesitol, triterpenoids: ursolic acid, lupeol acetate, flowers contain essential oils-β-linalool, cis-geraniol, trans-nerolidol, β-citronellol.	Fruits possess abortifacient properties. Leaves are crushed and given in stomach pains and diarrhoea. The root-bark is purgative, antiherpetic, useful in gonorrhoea and venereal sores. Bark is stimulant, decoction is useful in dropsical and venereal affection. Milky juice is applied to itches, rheumatism; also used as purgative.

Sl No.	Scientific Name	Local Name	Chemical Constituents	Medicinal uses
4.	***Jatropha curcas***	Physic nut (Awakege)	Leaves which show antileukemic activity contain a-amyrin, stigmasterol, campes3terol, beta-sitosterol and its derivatives, isovitexin and vitexin, presence of phorbol esters, the oil contain of seed is high (66.4%).	Leaf extract is used in toothache and promoting lactation. Latex is applied to boils and skin sores and also in rheumatism. Leaves are used for fumigating house to eradicate bed bugs.
5.	***Zanthoxylum acanthopodium***	Lemon pepper (Mukthrubi)	Aroma; Linalool; octyl acetate 56-β-cryophyllene. Protein: Fat; Fibre; Macro nutrient-K, Ca, Na, Micro nutrient-Fe, Zn, Cu, Mn, Cr.	Seeds and leaves are used in chronic fever, indigestion, cough and bronchitis. Oil extracted from the seeds is useful for healthy growth of hairs. Plant extract is used in the preparation of insecticides.

Sl No.	Scientific Name	Local Name	Chemical Constituents	Medicinal uses
6.	***Phlogacanthus thyrsiflorus***	Nongmangkha	Leaves-Quinazoline alkaloids vasicine-45-99% (the mucolytic drug bromhexine was developed from this alkaloid) N-oxides of vasicine, vasicinone, deoxyvasicine, oxyvasicinin, aiontone, essential oil. Flowers-b-sitosterol-D-glucoside, Kaempferol, glycosides of Kaempferoland, queretin. Roots vasicinolone, vasicol, peganine, hydroxy oxychalcone, glycosyl, oxychalcone.	Leaves are used in jaundice, asthma, muscular pains and rheumatic complaints. Leaves are insecticidal. Leaf-juice is used in diarrhoea, dysentery and glandular tumours. Powdered leaves are used for skin affections. Vasicine, is found to be urerotonic and abortifacient. Also used in stopping postpartum haemorrhage.
7.	***Parkia javanica***	Yongchak	Ripe seed contain 17.59% crude fat. The highest concentration of free phenols, ascorbic acid, crude fibre and ash wax in young, fully mature and ripe pods, respectively. Protein contents of dry young, fully mature and ripe seeds were 6.01, 23.04 and 22.26% respectively. In ripe seed, albumins plus globulins were 69.23% of the true protein.	Seeds are used in place of peppermint as a medicine for colic. Also used as anti-bacteria and is applied in traditional medicine for infections and stomach disorders.

Sl No.	Scientific Name	Local Name	Chemical Constituents	Medicinal uses
8.	***Acorus calamus***	Sweet flag (okhidak)	Alkaloids: Aroma: 1, 2, 4, Trimethoxy-5-prop-1-enyl-benzene: β-Asarone, linalool.	Rhizome is emetic, stomachic, used in dyspepsia, colic, remittent fevers, dysentery of children, insectifuge and in snake bite. Also used in epilepsy and other mental ailments, and glandular and abdominal tumours.
9	***Melia azedarcch***	Seijrak	The fruits of *M. azedarach* contains Melianoninol, melianol, melianone, meliandiol, vanillin, and vanillic acid. Presence of alkaloids, gum, resins, tannins, meliotanic acid. Their leaves contains flavonoid, phytosterols, Diterpene, alkane hydrocarbon, n-alkanic acid, vitamin E and Tri-Terpene alcohol.	*M. azedarach* is traditionally been used as anthelmintic, antilithic, diuretic, emmenagouge, astringent and stomachic. Various scienticfic studies reported the analgesic, anticancer, antioiral, antimalarial, antibacterial, antifeedant and antifertility activity of this plant.

Sl No.	Scientific Name	Local Name	Chemical Constituents	Medicinal uses
10.	**Ficus hispida**	Asi heibong	Preliminary phytochemical investigations of the F. hispida shown the presence of alkaloids, carbohydrates, proteins& amino acids, sterols, phenols, flavonoids, gums and mucilage, glycosides, saponins and terpenes. Apehnanthroindozidine alkaloid isolated m the CHCI3 extract of leaves and twings of F. hispida shown the presence of alkaloids, carbohydrates, proteins & amino acids, sterols, phenols flavonoids, gums and mucilage, glycosides saponins and terpens.	A pehnanthroindozidine alkaloid isolated from the chci3 extract of the leaves and twings of F. hispida was found to be active against small panel of human cancer cells. This compound has been characterized and named O. methylophorinidine

Tables

Table 1.1.a Occurrence of plant parasitic nematodes within Imphal West District of Manipur.

Sl. No.	Village	Crop	Nematode population/ 200 cm³ soil						
			Meloidogyne graminicola	*Helicotylenchus multieinetus*	*Tylenchorhynchus sp.*	*Pratylenchus sp.*	*Hoplaimus sp.*	*Xiphinema sp.*	*Criconematode sp.*
1	Malom	Maming thondabi	3060	1056				28	40
2	Maklang	K D		260				105	
3	Samurou Kobok loukol	Hemochandra			540	200			
4	Hiyangthang makha loukol	Tampha	50				1056		201
5	Meijrao loukol	RCM 9		1040			102		
6	Kakyai loukol	KD Angouba		1068		214		315	
7	Mekola loukol	Priya	1010		300			205	
8	Langpok Loukol	Thangjing				200			
9	Merakhong Loukol	Jatra	250				68		100
10	Lairenjam Loukol	KD			1055			215	
11	Konthoujam Loukol	Punshi	102				60		

Sl. No.	Village	Crop	Nematode population/ 200 cm³ soil						
			Meloidogyne graminicola	***Helicotylenchus multieinetus***	***Tylenchorhynchus sp.***	***Pratylenchus sp.***	***Hoplaimus sp.***	***Xiphinema sp.***	***Criconematode sp.***
12	Utlou Makha leikai	Jatra		105					
13	Phoijing	Ayangleima			250			260	
14	Nambol	Maming thondabi	44	1020					
15	Nambol thongkha	Lamyanba		2050		300		400	
16	Nambol Sabal Leikai	KD		1067		400		300	
17	Maibam Lokpa Ching	Jatra	408				508		
18	Oinam loukol	KD			540				
19	Erengbam loukol	Hemochandra		1050			20		10
20	Yaral Loukol	Jatra	950		340		105		20

Table 1.1.b Occurrence of plant parasitic nematodes within Imphal East District of Manipur.

Sl. No.	Village	Crop	Nematode population/ 200 cm³ soil						
			Meloidogyne graminicola	*Helicotylenchus multieinetus*	*Tylenchorhynchus sp.*	*Pratylenchus sp.*	*Hoplaimus sp.*	*Xiphinema sp.*	*Criconematode sp.*
1	Loijing maya Loubuk	Thangjing	50		87	43			
2	Loijing Ching Maya Loukon	K D angoubi		946					
3	Sinam lok Loukon	KD angoubi	44	230		54		34	
4	Yumalok Loukon	Phaungang			115		178		290
5	Checkon Loukon	Chabokpi	12423			69	100		250
6	Kanglou Loukon	Ayangleima	6614	500		45		65	
7	Ikop Loukon	Hemochandra			700		850		24
8	Thingel makha Loukon	Dharam	48		100				
9	Tairenpokpi Loukon	Jasra phou		4400		388		450	
10	Kharou Loukon	Nongin	135		550		450		800

Sl. No.	Village	Crop	Nematode population/ 200 cm³ soil						
			Meloidogyne graminicola	*Helicotylenchus multieinetus*	*Tylenchorhynchus sp.*	*Pratylenchus sp.*	*Hoplaimus sp.*	*Xiphinema sp.*	*Criconematode sp.*
11	Kongon toubi loukon	Khamba				750		500	
12	Nungoi loukon	Phoudum	200	100			250		300
13	Huidrom loukon	Jatra phou		2065			308		
14	Sawombung Loukon	Dharam	85		1020				
15	Hidumbi Loukon	KD angoubi		125		560		625	
16	Wairikhul loukon	Phaungang				1012			560
17	Mani yaiskul Loukon	Chabokpi	3400				540		100
18	Thamnapokpi Loukon	Hemochandra	25		150			5	
19	Bamon Loukon	Thangjing	120			50			400
20	Patlou Loukon	KD Amubi		1150			50		100

Table 1.1.c Occurrence of plant parasitic nematodes within Bishenpur District of Manipur.

Sl. No.	Village	Crop	Nematode population/ 200 cm³ soil						
			Meloidogyne graminicola	*Helicotylenchus multieinetus*	*Tylenchorhynchus sp.*	*Pratylenchus sp.*	*Hoplaimus sp.*	*Xiphinema sp.*	*Criconematode sp.*
1	Maibam Loukol	Hemochandra	150	28	84				10
2	Leimaram Lamkhai Loukol	Thangjing		1015		45			
3	Oinam Loukol	KD Amubi	64	200			48		34
4	Irengbam Loukol	KD Angoubi	1800		27	108			200
5	Keinou thongthak Loukol	KD Angoubi	45				102		34
6	Keinou thonkha Loukol	Phaungang	560		100		69		250
7	Keinou Maning Loukol	Thangjing	135	350		240	300	850	
8	Keinou Mamang Loukol	KD Amubi	1020		250				400
9	Ngaikhong Khun Loukol	Jatra phou	44	230		96	120		
10	Pumphou Loukol	Dharam			200			150	
11	Ngakchoupkpi Loukol	Phoudum	47		58	110			

Sl No.	Village	Crop	Nematode population/ 200 cm³ soil						
			Meloidogyne graminicola	***Helicotylenchus multieinetus***	***Tylenchorhynchus sp.***	***Pratylenchus sp.***	***Hoplaimus sp.***	***Xiphinema sp.***	***Criconematode sp.***
12	Chingdong Loukol	Khamba		1056				15	
13	Bishenpur Maning Loukol	Ayangleima			1012			600	45
14	Bishenpur Mamang Loukol	Nongin	2045		560	50		420	
15	Kwaksiphai Loukol	Phoungang			500				
16	Khoijuman Loukol	Thangjing				569	400		250
17	Potsangbam Loukol	KD Amubi	48		201			46	320
18	Nachou Loukol	Ayangleima		3050			500		200
19	Nachou Maning Loukol	Chabokpi		100		450			
20	Upokpi Loukol	Jatra Phou	45	250			140		

Table1.1.d Occurrence of plant parasitic nematodes within Thoubal District of Manipur.

Sl. No.	Village	Crop	Nematode population/ 200 cm^3 soil						
			Meloidogyne graminicola	*Helicotylenchus multieinetus*	*Tylenchorhynchus sp.*	*Pratylenchus sp.*	*Hoplaimus sp.*	*Xiphinema sp.*	*Criconematode sp.*
1	Khekman Loukol	Tampha	1345	1058		2010		50	20
2	Sanggaiyumpham Loukol	Dharam		560		110	240		120
3	Keibung Loukol	Tampha	46			450		670	1200
4	Wabgai Loukol	RCM 9				1058			
5	Khangabck Loukol	SK		560			700		480
6	Serou Loukol	Ayangleima	1020					520	
7	Phundrei Loukol	Jatra			450				600
8	Kakmayai Loukol	Maming thondabi	560		400			1040	
9	Heirok Loukol	Thangjing				550			670
10	Hiyanglam Loukol	Priya		1050			250		400
11	Tentha Loukol	Lamyanba			560				200
12	Thounaojam Loukol	RCM 9		2025				1020	
13	Irongchengsaba Loukol	SK	54					468	400
14	Khoirom Loukol	Ayangleima	150			100			200

SL No.	Village	Crop	Nematode population/ 200 cm³ soil						
			Meloidogyne graminicola	*Helicotylenchus multieinetus*	*Tylenchorhynchus sp.*	*Pratylenchus sp.*	*Hoplaimus sp.*	*Xiphinema sp.*	*Criconematode sp.*
15	Ichamkhunou Loukol	Jatra		250			300		150
16	Mantak Loukol	KD	100		20		56		50
17	Dolaithabi Loukol	SK	1175	1026				200	
18	Leisangthem Khong Maning Loukol	RCM 9		45		56		69	170
19	Leisangthem Khong Mamang Loukol	KD	40	120	65		102	560	
20	Leisangthem Khong Manung Loukol	Jatra	20	890		70	68		120

Table 1.1.e Community analysis of plant parasitic nematodes in different villages within Imphal West District of Manipur.

Sl. No.	Nematode	Absolute frequency	Relative frequency	Absolute density
1	*Meloidogyne graminicola*	4	16.67	146.85
2	*Helicotylenchus multicinetus*	4.5	18.75	217.9
3	*Tylenchorhynchus spp.*	3	12.5	75.62
4	*Pratylenchus spp.*	2.5	10.41	32.85
5	*Hoplolaimus spp.*	3.5	14.58	47.97
6	*Xiphinema spp.*	4	16.67	45.57
7	*Criconematode spp.*	2.5	10.41	9.275

Table 1.1.f Community analysis of plant parasitic nematodes in different villages within Imphal East District of Manipur.

Sl. No.	Nematode	Absolute frequency	Relative frequency	Absolute density
1	*Meloidogyne graminicola*	5.5	18.96	578.6
2	*Helicotylenchus multicinetus*	4	13.79	237.9
3	*Tylenchorhynchus spp.*	3.5	12.06	66.07
4	*Pratylenchus spp.*	4.5	15.5	74.27
5	*Hoplolaimus spp.*	4	13.79	68.15
6	*Xiphinema spp.*	3	10.34	41.97
7	*Criconematode spp.*	4.5	15.5	70.6

Table 1.1.g Community analysis of plant parasitic nematodes in different villages within Thoubal District of Manipur.

Sl. No.	Nematode	Absolute frequency	Relative frequency	Absolute density
1	*Meloidogyne graminicola*	5	15.87	112.75
2	*Helicotylenchus multicinetus*	5	15.87	189.6
3	*Tylenchorhynchus spp.*	2.5	7.93	37.37
4	*Pratylenchus spp.*	4	12.69	110.1
5	*Hoplolaimus spp.*	3.5	11.11	42.9
6	*Xiphinema spp.*	4.5	14.28	114.92
7	*Criconematode spp.*	7	22.22	119.5

Table 1.1.h Community analysis of plant parasitic nematodes in different villages within Bishenpur. istrict of Manipur.

Sl. No.	Nematode	Absolute frequency	Relative frequency	Absolute density
1	*Meloidogyne graminicola*	6	19.04	150.07
2	*Helicotylenchus multicinetus*	4.5	14.28	156.97
3	*Tylenchorhynchus spp.*	5	15.87	74.8
4	*Pratylenchus spp.*	4	12.69	41.7
5	*Hoplolaimus spp.*	4	12.69	41.97
6	*Xiphinema spp.*	3	9.52	52.02
7	*Criconematode spp.*	5	15.87	43.57

Table 1.3.a Screening of selected rice varieties against rice-knot nematode, *Meloidogyne graminicola* in Manipur.

Sl. No	Varieties	Root Length (cm)	Shoot Length (cm)	Fresh root weight (g)	Fresh shoot weight (g)	Dry root weight (g)	Dry shoot weight (g)	No. of seeds
1	Dharam	15	60	5.3	44	3.1	19	375
2	Tampha	14.3	59	5.2	42	2.7	18.4	340
3	RCM-9	13	57	5	38	2.3	18	290
4	SK	12.8	55	4.9	37	2.1	17.4	250
5	Ayangleima	12.4	53	4.7	34	2	17.2	240
6	Jatra	11.8	52.5	4.4	32	1.9	16	215
7	Mamingthondabi	11	52	4.1	30	1.8	16	195
8	Thangjing	10.9	51	3.8	27.5	1.5	15.4	170
9	Priya	10.6	50	3.6	25	1.3	15	150
10	Lamyanba	10	45	3.4	22	1	14.8	100

***The above given data is mean of three replication.**

Table 1.3.b Response of 10 varieties of rice to *Meloidogyne graminicola* under tub culture.

Sl. No	Varieties	Soil population	No. of galls	Root-Knot index	Root population	Total population	RF	Reaction
1	Dharam	101	2	1	20	121	0.03	Moderately Resistant
2	Tampha	375	5	1	25	400	0.08	Moderately resistant
3	RCM-9	800	14	2	85	885	0.17	Susceptible
4	SK	1000	18	2	120	1120	0.22	Susceptible
5	Ayangleima	2800	23	2	300	3100	0.62	Susceptible
6	Jatra	3200	30	3	750	3950	0.79	Susceptible
7	Mamingthondabi	4000	35	3	960	4960	0.9	Highly Susceptible
8	Thangjing	5400	35	3	1650	7050	1.41	Highly Susceptible
9	Priya	6800	40	3	2900	9700	1.94	Highly Susceptible
10	Lamyanba	7500	45	3	3500	11000	2.2	Highly Susceptible

*** The above data is mean of three replication.**

Table 2.3: a.i Evaluation of essential oils extracts of different medicinal plants on egg hatching of M. *graminicola.*

Plants	Duration (hr)	Percentage of hatching in dilution				
		0	1ppm	10ppm	100ppm	1000ppm
Vitex negundo	12	23	4.2	3	1	0
	24	34	6.5	5	3	1
	48	42	8.4	7.2	5.2	3
Jatropha curcas	12	20	3.5	1	0	0
	24	32	5.4	3	1	0
	48	38	7.4	5.3	4.2	2
Plumeria acutifolia	12	51	31	25	18	15
	24	68	42	32	21	17
	48	82	56	45	28	20
Phlogacanthus thyrsiflorus	12	46	27	18	12	11
	24	62	31	24	15	13
	48	71	42	31	20	16
Melia azedarach	12	28	5.5	4.5	2	1
	24	40	7.6	6.2	4	2
	48	50	9	8.4	6.1	4
Zanthoxylum acanthopodium	12	30	7.4	5.4	3.4	2
	24	41	8.5	7.1	5.2	4
	48	52	10.2	9.2	7.2	6
Tagetes patula	12	15	2.3	0	0	0
	24	28	3.8	2.1	0	0
	48	41	6.5	4.5	3.1	1
Ficus hispida	12	43	21	15	10.1	10
	24	56	28	20	13.4	12.5
	48	68	32	27	18.5	14.5
Parkia javanica	12	35	8.9	6.1	5.2	4
	24	46	10.4	9.4	7.8	6
	48	57	13.5	10.1	9.2	7.5
Aerorus calamus	12	38	12	10.4	7.8	5
	24		15.5	13.2	9.5	7.1
	48		20.3	18	16	12.1

* The result is mean of three replications.

Table 2.3: a.ii Evualuation of essential oil extracts of different medicinal plants on larval mortality of *M. gramnicola*.

Plants	Duration	Percentage of Mortality in dilution				
		0	1ppm	10ppm	100ppm	1000ppm
Tagetes patula	12	3.4	40.5	80.4	97.8	100
	24	3.4	55.3	88.4	100	100
	48	3.4	82.1	95.3	100	100
Jatropha curcus	12	3.4	34.8	77.8	86.4	98.5
	24	3.4	50.4	85.3	97.4	100
	48	3.4	73.4	91.4	100	100
Aerorus calamus	12	3.4	33.1	70.3	80.4	95.3
	24	3.4	45.4	83.2	90.2	100
	48	3.4	65.2	88.4	95.8	100
Melia azedarach	12	3.4	30.1	65.2	78.2	93.1
	24	3.4	40.3	75.4	80.1	95.4
	48	3.4	60.1	80.4	90.1	100.4
Phlogacanthus thyrsiflorus	12	3.4	25.1	50.3	75.1	90.3
	24	3.4	35.4	70.3	75.1	95.6
	48	3.4	53.4	75.3	86.4	98.4
Vitex negundo	12	3.4	23.5	45.6	72.3	85.4
	24	3.4	30.1	53.2	65.4	85.4
	48	3.4	50.3	68.3	79.4	95.3
Parkia javanica	12	3.4	20.4	43.2	70.1	80.4
	24	3.4	28.3	50.1	60.1	81.2
	48	3.4	48.2	65.1	75.2	90.1
Zanthoxylum acanthopodium	12	3.4	18.4	40.2	65.1	78.2
	24	3.4	25.1	48.2	58.3	82.2
	48	3.4	45.1	63.2	73.1	86.3
Plumeria acutifolia	12	3.4	17.3	38.2	63.1	75.4
	24	3.4	23.1	46.1	53.6	80.4
	48	3.4	43.1	62.1	72.3	84.5
Ficus hispida	12	3.4	16.3	35.1	57.1	74.5
	24	3.4	20.1	40.1	52.1	78.2
	48	3.4	40.3	54.5	68.2	82.6

Table 2.3.b.i Effect of oil extract of medicinal plants against rice root knot nemoatode infecting rice plant Dharam. in plant growth parameters.

Medicinal Plants	Root Length (cm)	Shoot Length (cm)	Fresh Shoot wt. (g)	Fresh Root wt. (g)	Dry Shoot wt. (g)	Dry Root wt. (g)	Number Of grains
P. javanica	5.96	30.5	8.99	3.01	6.77	1.45	41
X. acanthopodium	5.76	30.46	8.82	2.9	6.50	1.02	39
J. curcas	6.54	33.7	11.9	4.18	9.67	2.86	56
V. negundo	5.52	31	10.5	3.56	8.09	1.07	45
P. thyrsiflorus	5.99	32.1	10.9	3.98	8.87	1.91	48
Control	3.76	29	7.99	2.04	5.77	1.01	35

Table 2.3.b.ii Effect of oil extract of medicinal plants on nematode population against root knot nematode infecting Dharam local rice variety.

Medicinal Plants	Number of Galls/ plant	Soil pop. (500 g of soil)	Root pop. /plant	Root knot Index	Total Pop.	Rf
P. javanica	13	580	460	2	1040	1.04
X. acanthopodium	16	880	430	2	1310	1.31
J. curcas	7	360	220	1	580	0.58
V. negundo	10	790	320	2	1110	1.11
P. thyrsiflosus	9	430	390	1	820	0.82
Control	23	920	770	3	1690	1.69

Table 2.3.c.i Evaluation of essential oil extracts of medicinal plants against rice root knot nematodes infecting rice plant Tampha in plant growth parameters.

Medicinal Plants	Root length (cm)	Shoot length (cm)	Fresh shoot wt. (g)	Fresh root wt. (g)	Dry shoot wt. (g)	Dry root wt. (g)	No. of grains
Tagetes patula	7.12	41.2	12.3	5.21	10.1	2.5	64
Ficus hispicla	5.21	32.5	9.5	2.52	7.2	1.30	40
Acrorus calamus	6.54	35.2	11.4	4.12	9.1	2.1	56
Plumeria acutifolia	5.41	30.42	10.9	2.98	8.4	1.40	45
Melia azedarach	6.13	34.3	11.2	3.94	8.9	1.56	48
Control	4.24	30	8.5	2.12	6.2	1.1	30

* *The results are mean of three replicates*

Table 2.3.c.ii Evaluation of essential oil extracts of medicinal plants on nematodes population against root knot nematode infects on Tampha local rice variety.

Medicinal Plants	Numbers of galls/ plants	Soil population (100g of soil)	Root population/ plant	Root Knot index	Total population	RF
Tagetes patula	6	320	210	1	530	0.53
Ficus hispicla	16	910	456	2	1366	1.3
Acrorus calamus	8	400	230	1	630	0.63
Plumeria acutifolia	13	750	370	2	1120	1.1
Melia azedarach	10	540	310	2	850	0.85
Control	25	950	810	3	1760	1.76

* *The results are mean of three replicates*

Graphs

Graph: Occurrence of rice root knot nematode in different rice varieties in four plan districts of Manipur.

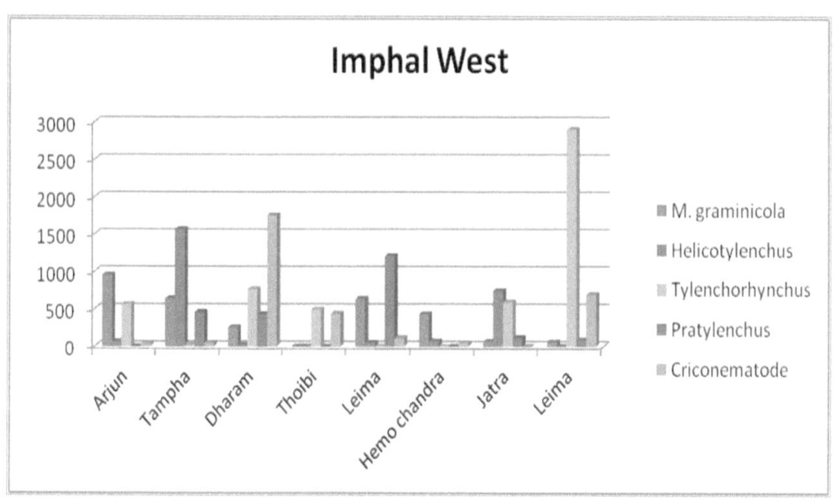

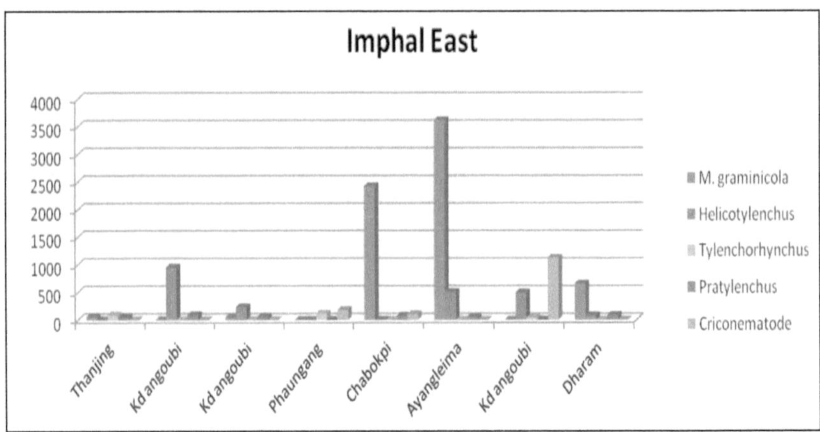
Imphal East
4000
3500
3000
2500
2000
1500
1000
500
0
Thanjing
Kd angoubi
Kd angoubi
Phaungang
Chabokpi
Ayangleima
Kd angoubi
Dharam
M. graminicola
Helicotylenchus
Tylenchorhynchus
Pratylenchus
Criconematode

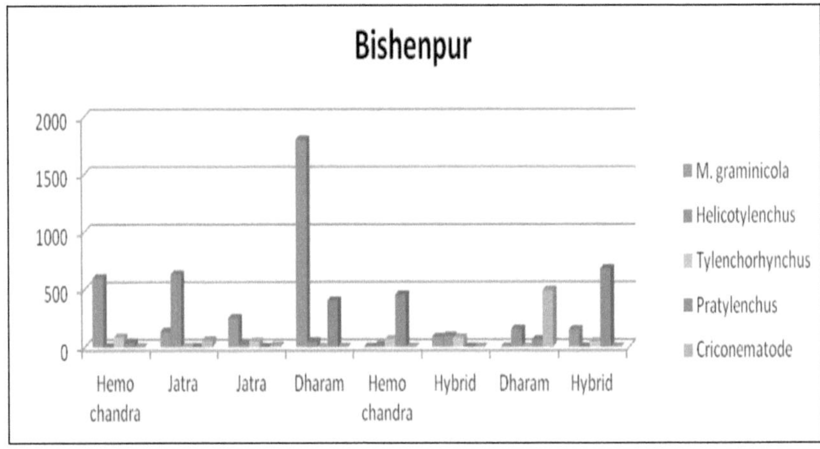
Bishenpur
2000
1500
1000
500
0
Hemo chandra
Jatra
Jatra
Dharam
Hemo chandra
Hybrid
Dharam
Hybrid
M. graminicola
Helicotylenchus
Tylenchorhynchus
Pratylenchus
Criconematode

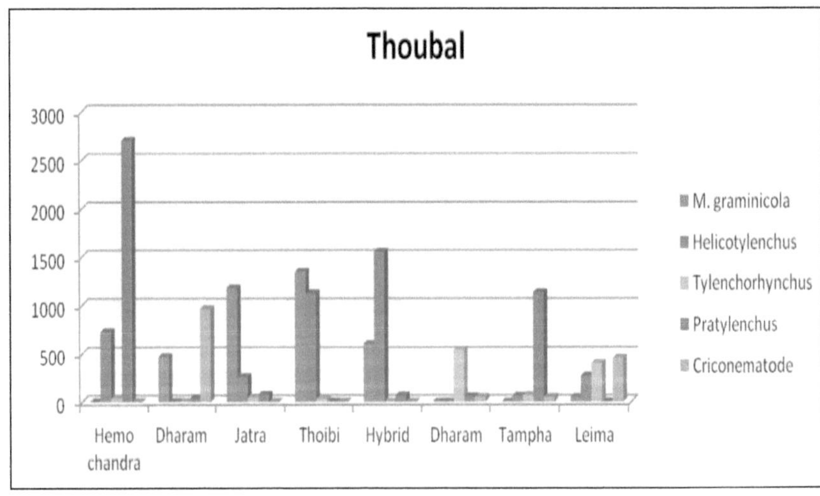
Thoubal
3000
2500
2000
1500
1000
500
0
Hemo chandra
Dharam
Jatra
Thoibi
Hybrid
Dharam
Tampha
Leima
M. graminicola
Helicotylenchus
Tylenchorhynchus
Pratylenchus
Criconematode

Graph 1.2.a. Screening of selected rice varieties against rice-knot nematode, *Meloidogyne graminicola* in Manipur.

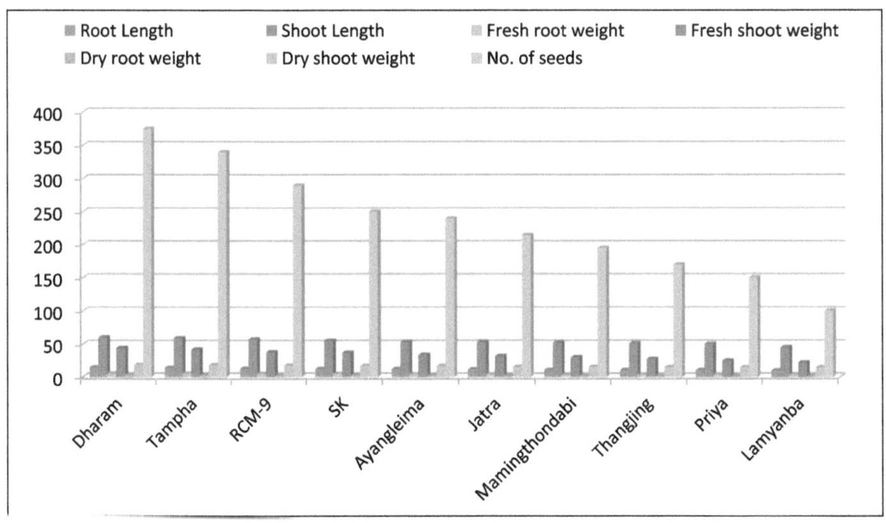

Graph 1.2.b. Response of 10 varieties of rice to *Meloidogyne graminicola* under tub condition.

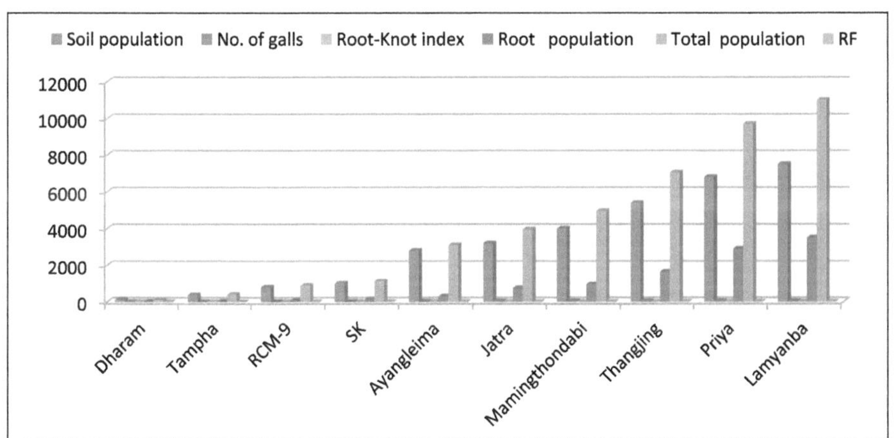

Graph 2.3.a.i Rate of egg hatching at 12 hours exposure period.

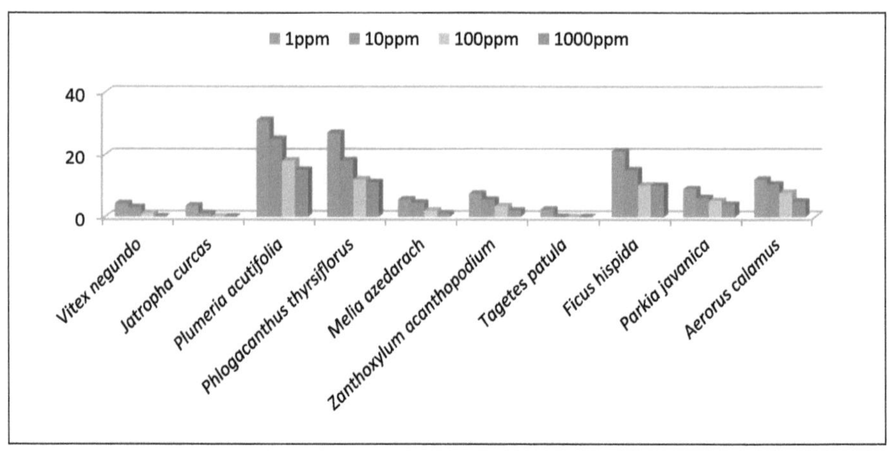

Graph 2.3.a.i Rate of egg hatching at 24 hours exposure period.

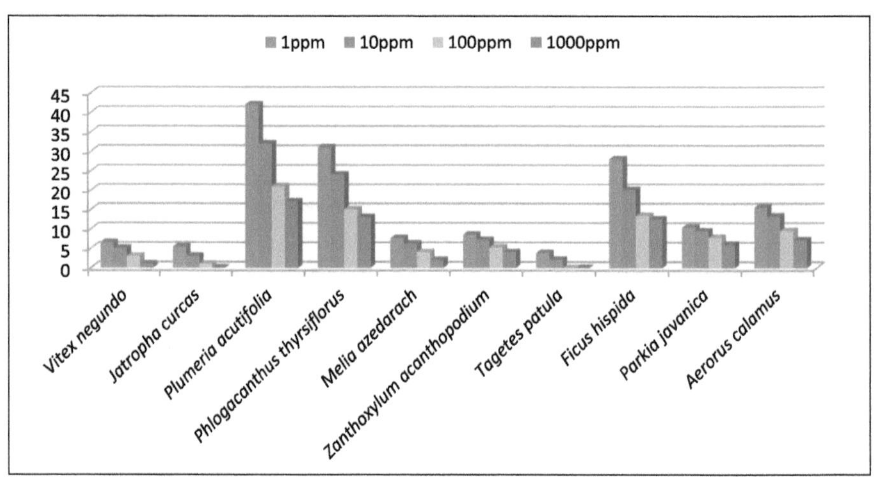

Graph 2.3.a.i Rate of egg hatching at 48 hours exposure period.

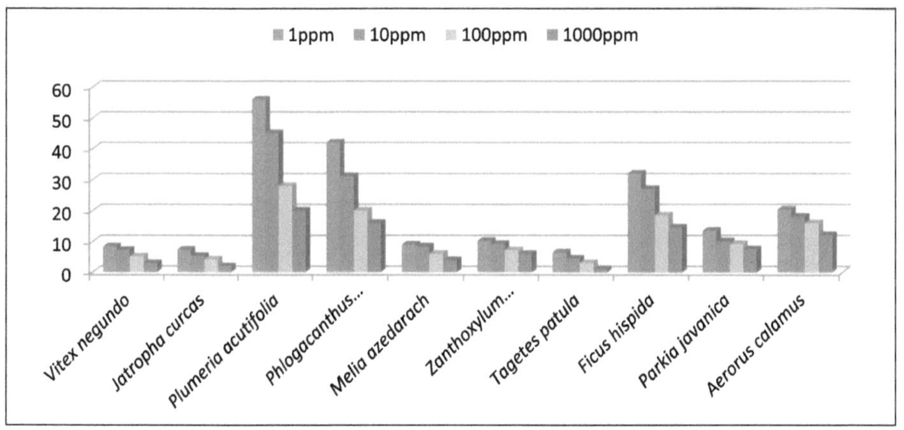

Graph 2.3.a.ii Rate of Mortality at 12 hours exposure period.

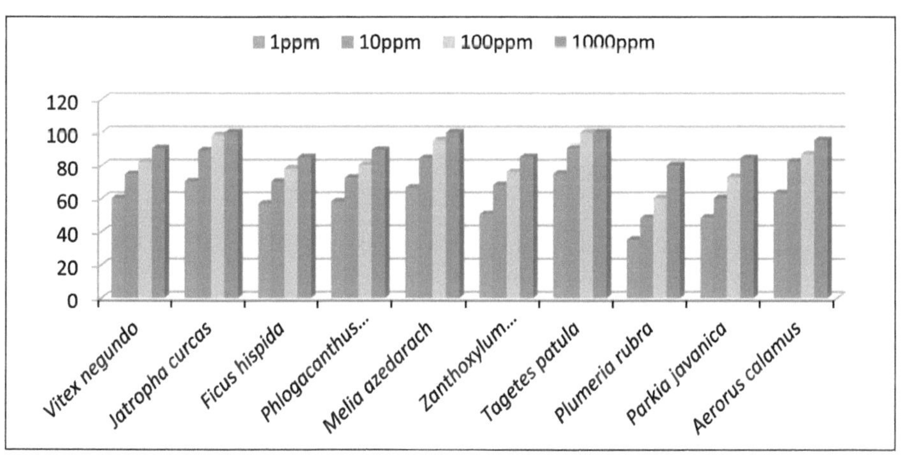

Graph 2.a.ii. Rate of Mortality at 24 hours exposure period.

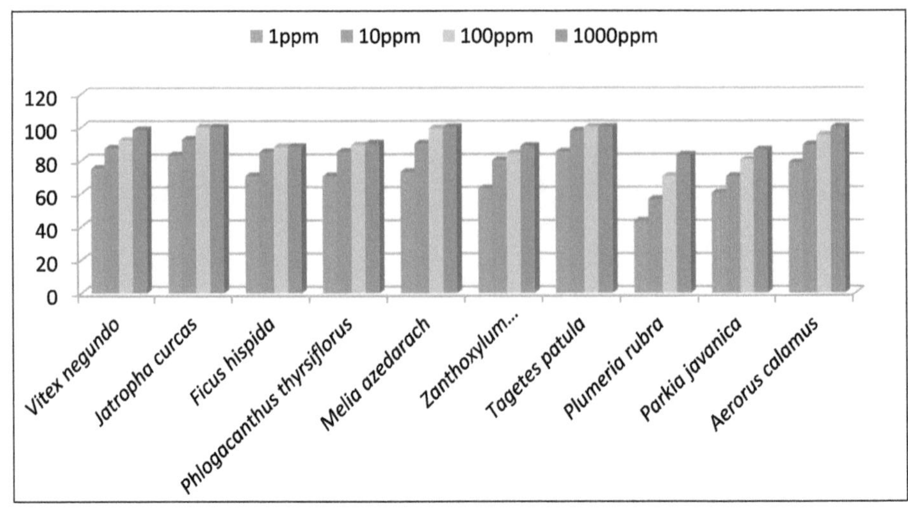

Graph 2.a.ii. Rate of Mortality at 48 hours exposure period.

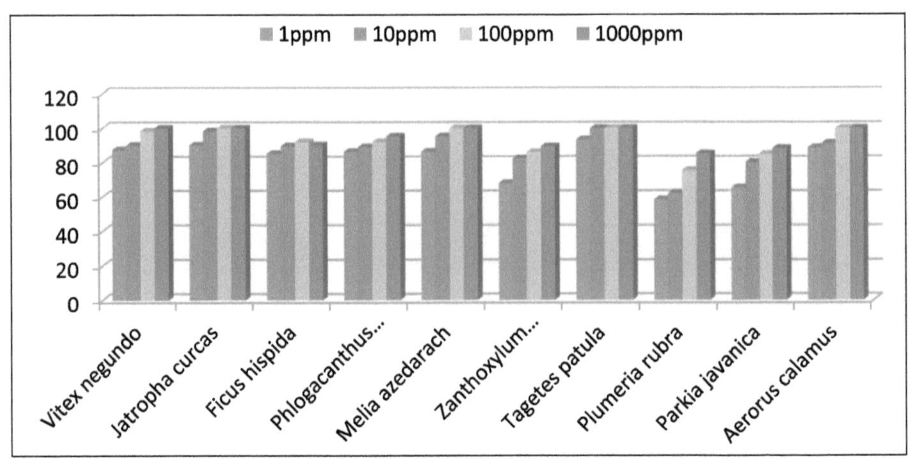

Graph 2.3.b.i. Effect of oil extract of medicinal plants against rice root knot nemoatode infecting rice plant Dharam. in plant growth parameters.

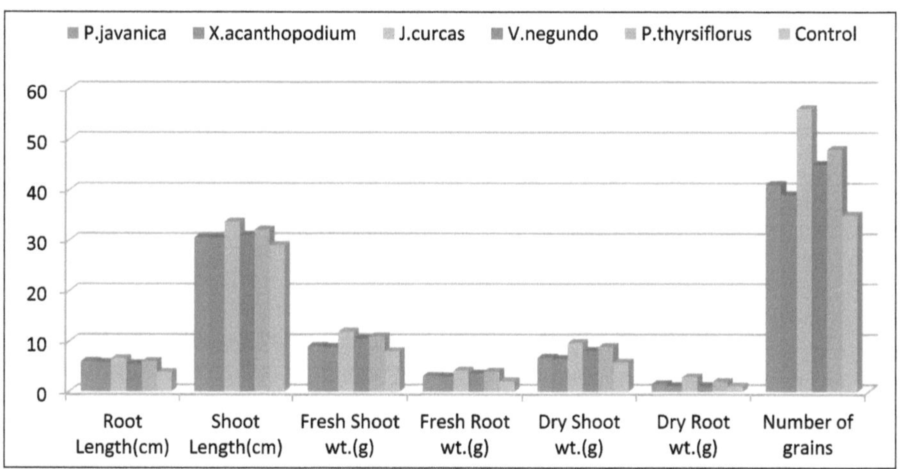

Graph 2.3.b.ii Effect of oil extract of medicinal plants on nematode population against root knot nematode infecting Dharam local rice variety.

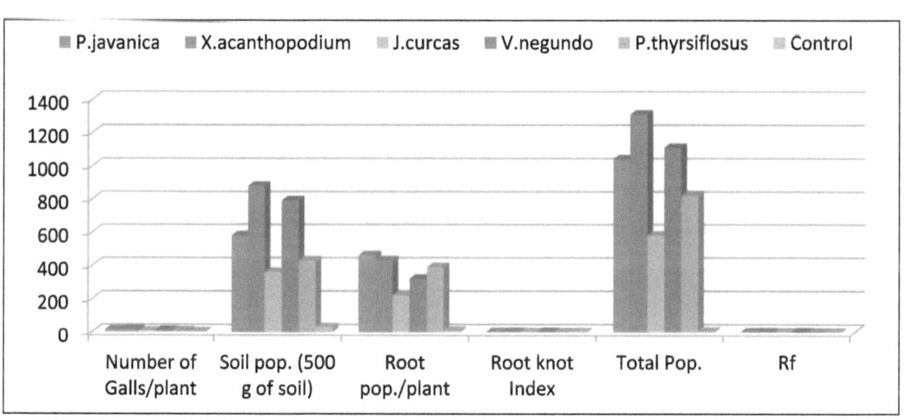

Graph 2.3.c.i Evaluation of essential oil extracts of medicinal plants against rice root knot nematodes infecting rice plant Tampha in plant growth parameters.

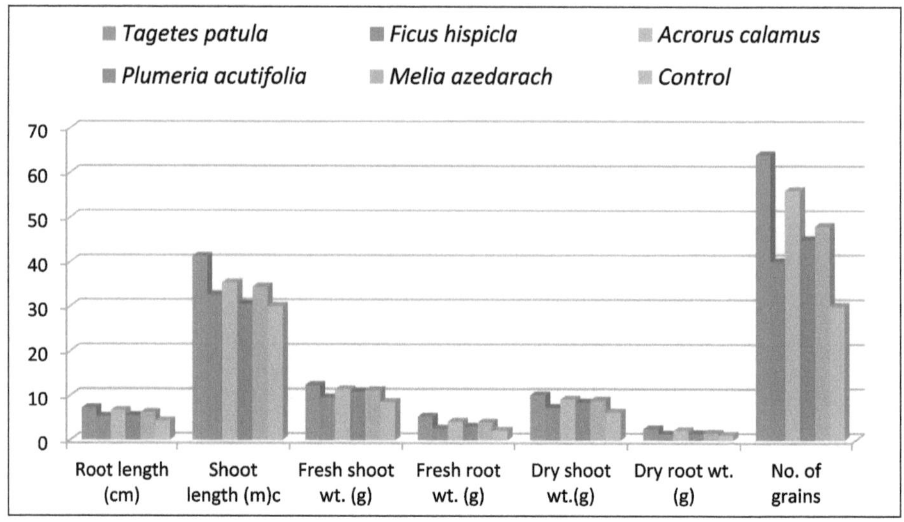

Graph 2.3.c.ii Evaluation of essential oil extracts of medicinal plants on nematodes population against root knot nematode infects on Tampha local rice variety.

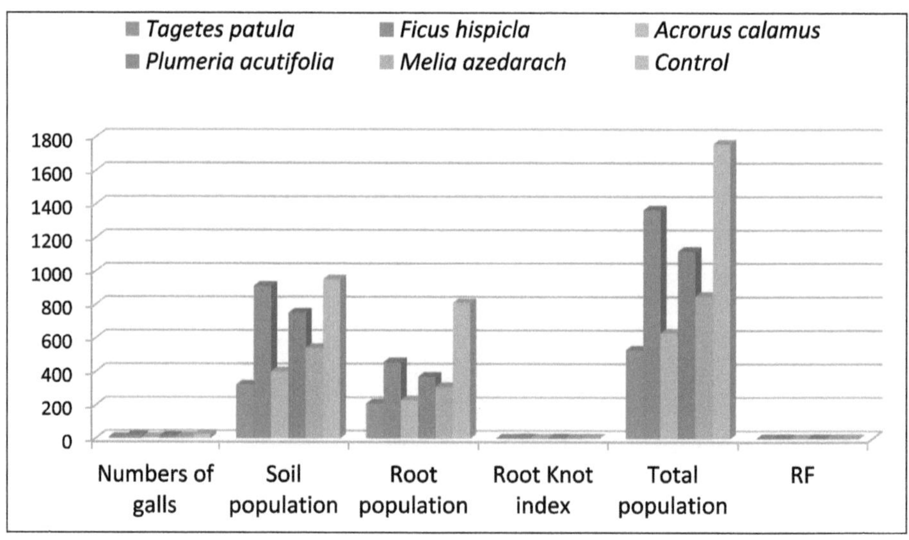

Photos

Root knot nematode *Meloidogyne incognita*

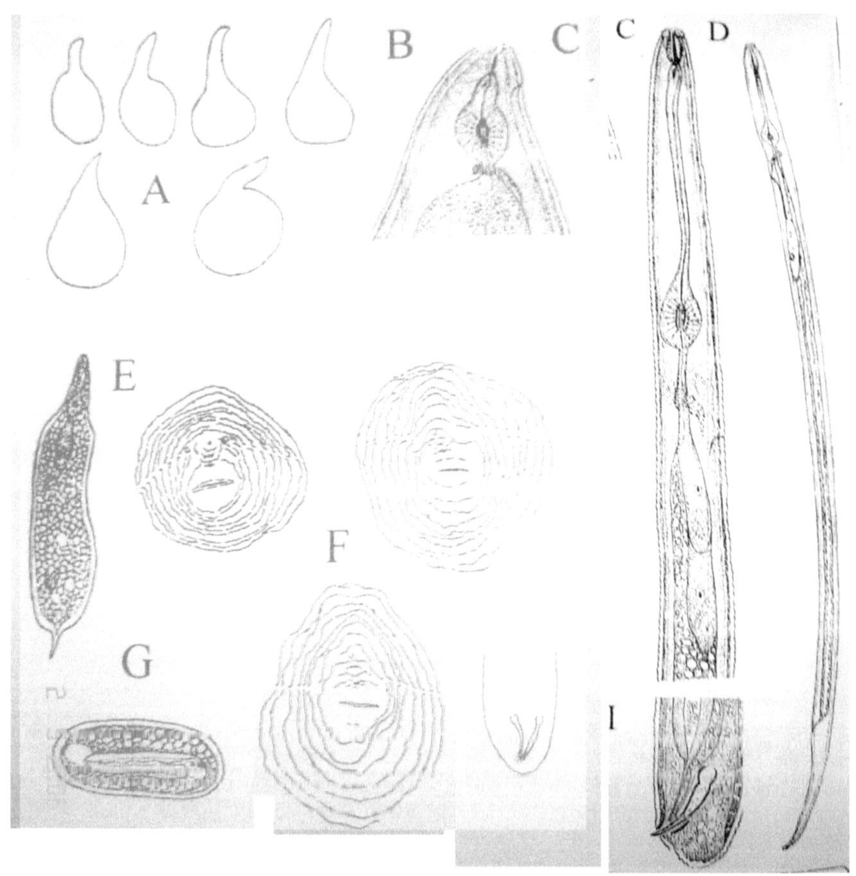

A – Female, B- Head of Female, E – 3rd stage Juvenile, G – Egg
F – Perrinial Patterial, C & D – Male, I – Male Tail

Root knot nematode *Meloidogyne graminicola*

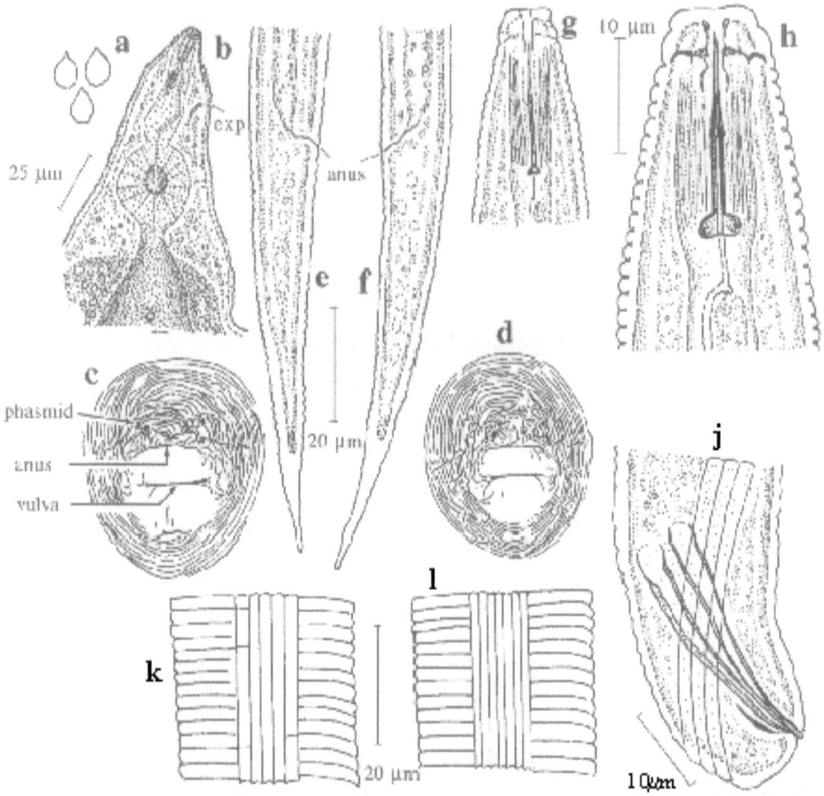

(a)female; (b) (exp) excretory pore; (c) and (d) perineal pattern; (e) and (f) second stage juvenile tail;
(g) second stage juvenile with delicate stylet; (h) male; (j) lateral fields in young males; (k) and (l) lateral fields in mature males

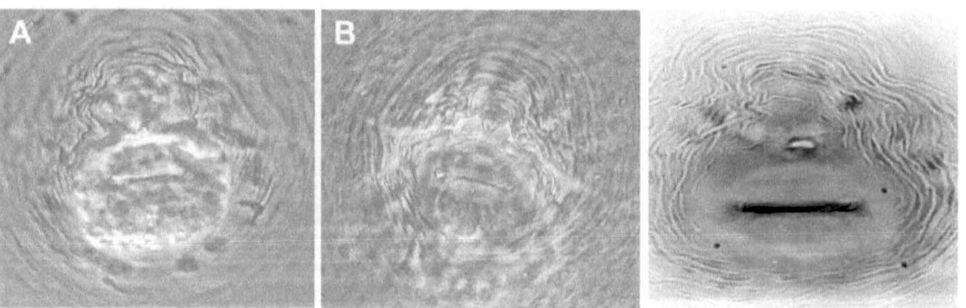

Perrenial pattern of	**Perrenial pattern of**
M. graminicola	***M. incognita***

Field Survey Photo

Infected field of brinjal at Kakyai (Bishenpur District)

Infected root of brinjal at the kakyai (Bishenpur District) during the survey

Infected field of rice and the root infestation at Heirok (Thoubal District)

Some selected photographs of survey work with P.I and Research Scholars

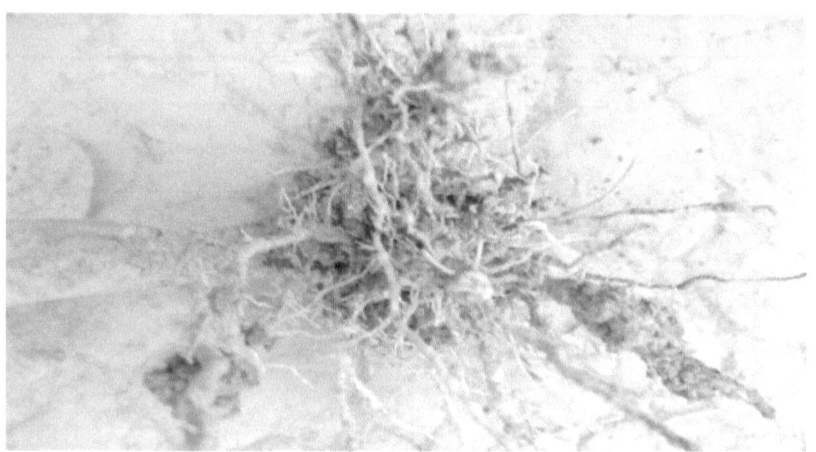

Infected plant of brinjal with
M. incognita

Infected plant of rice with
M. graminicola

TEN SELECTED MEDICINAL PLANTS TO BE TESTED

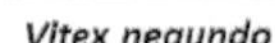

Vitex negundo

Jatropha curcas

Plumaria acutifolia

Phlogacanthus thyrsiformis

Zanthoxylum acanthopodium

Melia azedarach

Tagetes patula

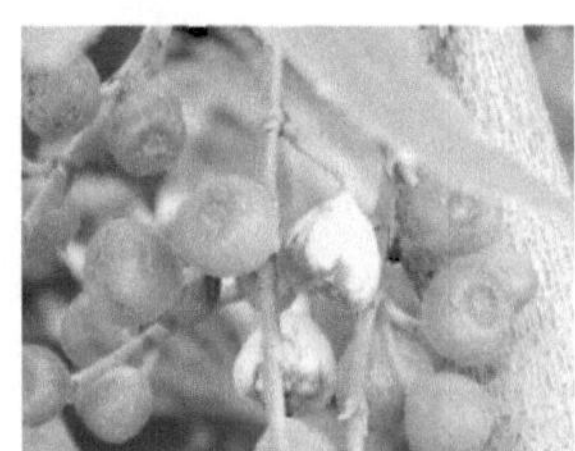

Ficus hispida

Parkia javanica

Acrorus calamus

Experimental tub with rice varieties

Injected plant of rice with *M. graminicola*

ONE DAY TRAINNING PROGRAMME

COLLECTION OF MEDICINAL PLANTS

PREPARATION OF ESSENTIAL OIL USING CLEVENGER APPARATUS

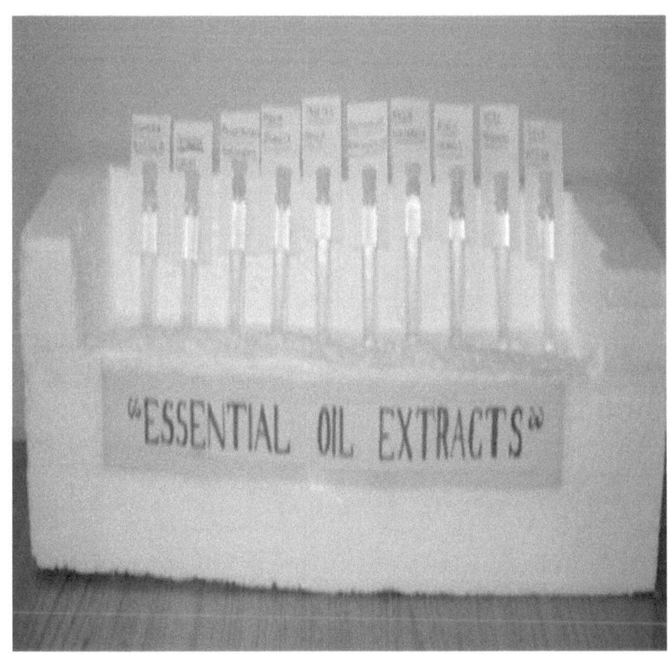

Essential oil extracts from the 10 selected medicinal plants

Summary

The root knot nematode *Meloidogyne spp.* Constitute the most important group of nematode pests of majority of the agricultural crops. Antinemic properties of different plant products have been thoroughly exploited by many Indian nematologists and tried out in various forms. In Manipur several indigenous medicinal plants are grown which possess antinemic properties but no such attempt was done for their utility as oil products against root knot nematode in different ways. The present work mainly deals with two chapters-

Chapter number one deals with many ecological studies of rice plants infested with root knot nematode *Meloidogyne graminicola* as follows:-

1.1 Survey on incidence of rice root knot nematode on different rice fields of Manipur

A preliminary survey of rice root knot nematode from July 2012 upto October 2014 was conducted in different four plain districts of Manipur they are Imphal East, Imphal west, Bisnupur and Thoubal Districts. Out of 250 different villages surveyed only 80 localities were selected from the four plain districts of Manipur. In this survey altogether 41 localities were foud infested with rice root knot nematode. but there were varying of their disease incid ence. Some of plants were seriously infected with these pest but some have low disease infestation rate. Field survey revealed that *M. graminicola* was widely distributed in most rice growing areas of four plain districts of Manipur. Rice root knot disease was more prevalent in dry bed condition than wet bed condition. Most of the farmers grew seedlings in upland (dry) soiland there was more rice root knot disease and second stage juvenile population in both nursery and seedling root. The galled (diseased) seedling had significantly shorter roots and shoots. Most of the farmers did not know about the nematode problem and did not follow any management practices to control it in nurseries and in the main field. This indicated high risk of multiplication of the nematodes and huge lost in rice production. Altogether seven plant parasitic nematode genera viz. *M. graminicola, Helicotylenchus multicintus, Tylenchorhynchus sp, Pratylenchus sp, Hoplolaimus sp, Xiphinema sp,* and *Criconematodes sp,* were found associated with different varieties of rice during this investigation. Although several plant parasitic nematodes are encounterd with rice root knot nematode but frequently encountered genera of six types was only selected. The highest number of *M. graminicola* (12423) was recorded in chabokpi variety of rice at Checkon loukon of paurabi followed by Kanglou loukon (6614) of Imphal East. Next to it is the Maniyaiskul loukon (3400) of Imphal East, Malom loukol (3060) of Imphal west, Checkon loukon (2423) of Imphal East, Bishenpur mamang loukon (2045) of Bisnupur District, Irengbam loukon (1800) of Bisnupur, Kheckman loukol (1345) of Thoubal District, Dolaithabi loukol (1175) of Thoubal District, Serou loukol (1020) of Thoubal District, Mekola loukol (1010) of Imphal west district, Yaral loukol (950) of Imphal west district, Kakmayai loukol (560) of Thoubal district, Maibam lokpa ching (408) of Imphal west, Maibam loukol (150) of Bisnupur District, Kharou loukol (135) of Imphal East, Bamon loukol (120) of Imphal east, Utlou loukol (102) of Imphal west.

1.2 Identification of root knot nematode up to their species level

Meloidogyne spp. belongs to family Heteroderidae. The root knot nematodes were first named by Cornu 1879 in France. White Head 1968 reviewed the genus *Meloidogyne* and confirmed the distinctive morphological characters of 23 species of *Meloidogyne*. In this present studies many specimen of root knot nematode were found and the specimen were identified as *Meloidogyne incognita* and *Meloidogyne graminicola* based on the perennial cuticular pattern of gravid female. The concerned root knot nematode was identified as *Meloidogyne incognita* and *Meloidogyne graminicola.*

Meloidogyne incognita and *Meloidogyne graminicola* is widely distributed in Manipur along with a wide range of host. The measurements and morphological characters of the present populations are similar with those dimensions given by Orton (1973), Eisenback (1985), Hirchmann (1985), Jairajpuri and Baqri (1991). But the present male specimens have slightly shorter stylet and gubernaculums.

1.3 Host range studies of rice root knot nematode in different varieties of rice crops of Manipur

Screening of some common rice varieties of Manipur were tested for their resistance against rice root-knot nematode *(Meloidogyne graminicola).* The investigation was conducted on 10 ricei varieties, which showed evidence of damaging potential of *Meloidogyne graminicola* in terms of plant growth parameters and disease incidence. Disease intensity grade was classified on the basis of root knot index. All the varieties were susceptible to *Meloidogyne graminicola* except Dharam and Tampha which were moderately resistant. Maximum number of root galls (45) were recorded in rice variety Lamyanba whereas minimum root galls (2) were recorded in rice variety Dharam.

Chapter number two deals with management studies as follows:

2.3 (a) Laboratory Condition

Efficacy of essential oil extracts obtained from the selected 10 medicinal plants against egg hatching and larval mortality of *M. graminicola*

Rice is the stable food of the country after wheat and largest cultivated area among all food grains in India. *Meloidogyne graminicola* is a serious pest of rice and causing extensive damage to rice crop in many countries of the world including India. For several decades the management of plant parasite nematodes has been mainly dominated by the use of synthetic chemical nematicides. But their application is problematic because of many negative environmental impacts and consequently many good nematicides have been withdrawn from the market. Therefore, there is a strong demand to develop more sustainable and environmentally benign method for nematodes control. The objective of this study is to assess the nematicidal effectiveness of essential oils from ten selected medicinal plants. viz. *Vitex negundo, Jatropha curcus, Plumeria acutifolia, Phlogacanthus thyrsiflorus, Mellia azedarach, Zanthoxylum acanthopodium, Tagetes patula, Ficus hispida, Parkia javanica and Acrorus calamus* aginst eggs of *Melioidogyne graminicola* in terms of eggs hatching and larval mortality. Egg hatching was maximum in control, although among the ten medicinal plant tested, essential oil extracts obtained from *Tagetes patula* shows most inhibitory effect followed by *Jatropha curcas* extracts. Rate of hatching was inversely proportional with concentration of extracts and directly with exposure period but in case of larval mortality it was directly proportional with concentration of extracts as well as duration of exposure period. Extract from *Ficus hispida* was found least effective among treated plants.

2.3 (b) Pot experiments

Efficacy of essential oil extracts of medicinal plants gainst rice root knot nematode *Meloidogyne graminicola* in pots

A tub experiment was conducted to study the efficacy of essential oil extracts of medicinal plants against *Meliodogyne graminicola* on common rice variety Dharam. Essential oil extracts obtained from five selected medicinal plants viz. *Parkia javanica, Zanthoxylum acanthopodium, Jatropha curcas, Vitex negundo* and *Adatoda vasica* were tested as seed soaking against rice root knot nematode. The seeds were soaked in 100ppm concentration for 24 hours. The plants treated with essential oil extract of *Jatropha curcas* showed improvement in plant growth and reduction in diseases incidence when compared with other treated plants. Essential oil extracts of *Zanthoxylum acanthopodium* was found to be least effective among five tested plants.

2.3 (c) Evaluation of essential oils of medicinal plants against rice root knot pest in Manipur

Evaluation of essential oils obtained from 5 different medicinal plants viz. *Tagetes patula, Ficus hispida, Acrorus calamus, Plumeria acutifolia and Melia azedarach* against rice root knot nematode *Meloidogyne graminicola* on common rice variety Tampha was conducted in tub experiment from 1st May 2012 upto 30th Sept. 2013 at the lawn of P.G. Department of Zoology D.M. college of Science Imphal. The seeds were soaked in 100ppm concentration for 24 hours. Essential oil extracts obtained from *Tagetes patula* showed most effective which showed improvement in plant growth and reduction in disease incidence followed by extracts from *Acrorus calamus* treated plants when compared with other treatment plants. Essential oil extracts obtained from *Ficus hispida* was found to be least effective among five tested plants.

References

Abad Pierse & Patric Wincker (2008). Genome sequence of he metazoan plant parasitic nematode *M. incognita*. ***Nature Biotechnology 26 (8):*** 909-915.

Amoussou P.L., Ashurt J., Green J., Jones M., Koyama M., Snape J.T.W. and Atkinson H., (2004), Broadly based resistance to nematodes in the rice and potato crops of subsistence farmers. Pp. 9-14. *DFID Plant Sciences Research Programme Annual Report, 2004.*

Anamika, simon, S and Singh, R.K. (2011) occurrence of root knot disease in green onion in Allahabad. Archv. Phytopathol.Pi. Protec.44.101-104.

Anil Prashar, Thaman S., Humphreys E., Yadvinder S., Nayyar A., Gajri P.R., Dhillon S.S. and Jagadish T., (2004). Performance of rice on beds and puddled transplanted flats in Punjab, India. 4th International Crop Science Congress. 26 September – 1 October, 2004. Brisbane, Queensland, Australia, Poster No. 570.

Ali, S.S. (1989). Occurrence of plant parasitic nematodes associated with pulse crops. ***National symposium on New Frontiers in Pulses Research and Development. Dte. of Pulses Res., Kanpur, Abstr.*** pp. 28.

Ali, S.S. and Kosshy, P.K. (1982) Occurrence of root knot nematode in Cardamon plantation of Kerala. ***Nematol. Medit 10***: 107-110.

Alvarez Castellanos PP, Bishop CD, Pascula-Villalobes MJ (2001). Antifungal activity of the essential oil of flower heads of garland chrysanthemum against agricultural pathogens. ***Phytochemistry 57***, 99-102.

A.O.A.C (1980). Official methods of analysis, 13th Ed. ***Association of official analytical chemist, Washington D.C.*** 376-384.

Bajaj, H.K. & Jairajpuri, M.S. (1979). A review of the genus *Xiphinema* Cobb, 1913 with descriptions of species from India. ***Rec. Zool. Surv. India*** 75:

Bridge J, L Michel and Plowright. (1990). Nemtode parasites of rice. In Plant parasitic nematodes in subtropical and tropical agriculture (M Lue, RA Sikora and J Bridge, eds). UK, CAB International. Pp. 69-108316-317.

Baqri, Q.H.; Baqri, S.Z. and Jairajpuri, M.S. (1978). Studies on *Mononchida*, two new species of *Iotonchus, Cobbonchus indicus n. sp.* and *Anatonchus ginglymodonties mulvey* 1961. ***Nematologica*** 24: 436-444.

Barber, C.A. (1901). A tea eel worm disease in South India. ***Tropical Agriculturist*** 21: 238.

Bhagavati, B. And Bora. S.C. (2001). A new record of root knot nematode, *Meloidogyne incognita* infecting *Amaranthus blitum* in Assam. ***Indian J. Nematology***. 31 (1): 94.

Bhatti, D.S. and Dahiya, R.S. (1977). New host records of *Meloidogyne* spp. ***Indian J. Nematology.*** 7 (2). 154.

Bridge J, L Michel and Plowright. (1990). Nemtode parasites of rice. In Plant parasitic nematodes in subtropical and tropical agriculture (M Lue, RA Sikora and J Bridge, eds). UK, CAB International. Pp. 69-108.

Bridge, J. and S.L.J. Page (1982). The Rice root knot nematode *M. graminicola* on deep water rice (Oryza sativa sub sp. Indica) ***Rev.de Nematol.***5: 225-232.

Bhatti, D.S. & Jain, R.K. (1977). Estimation of losses in okra, tomato, and brinjal yield due to *Meloidogyne incognita*. ***Indian J. Nematology***. 7: 37-41.

Bora, B.C. and P.P. Neog (2006). Effect of oilcakes for management of *Meloidogyne incognita* on tea.*Ann. Pl.Protec.Sci.* **14**: 522-523.

Buena, A.P., Diez-Rojo, M.A., Lopez-Perez, J.A., Roberton, L. Eseuer, M. and Bello, A. (2007) Screeting of *Tagetes patula,* on different populations of *Meloidogyne*. Crop protection *27: 96-100.*

Butter, E.J. (1913). Disease of rice. An eelworm disease of rice. ***Agri. Res. Inst. Pasa. Bull***. 34: 1-27.

Carvatho, J.M.F.C.; Ferraz, S.; Cardosa, A.A. and Dhingra, O.D. (1981). Treatment of Phaseolus vulgaris seeds with examyl dissolved in acetone or ethanol for the control of Phytonematodes. ***Revista Ceris***. 28: 580-587.

Chandravadana, M.U.; Sebastian, E.; Nidiery, J.; Lella, N.K.; Parvatha Reddy, P.; Khan, R.M. and Rao, M.S. (1996). Nematicidal activity of some plant extracts. ***Indian J. Nematology.*** 26 (2): 148-151.

Chitra, S and Dhyani, S.K. (2006). Insect pest of *Jatropha curcas*L. and the potential for their management. Current cience 91: 162-163.

Chitwood, B.G. (1949). Root-knot nematodes Part I, Revision of the genus Meloidogyne Goeldi 1887. ***Proceedings of Helminthology Society, Washington*** 16: 90-104.

Chitwood, D.J. (2002). Ann. Rev. ***Phytopathol***. 40: 221-49.

Chopra, R.N.; Nayar, S.L. and Chopra, I.C. (1956). Glossary of Indian Medicinal plants. ***C.S.I.R. New Delhi***. 330 pp.

Cobb, N.A. (1918). Estimating the nema population of the soil. ***Agri. Tech. Circ. Bur. Pl. Ind. U.S. Dep. Agric.*** No.1.

Cornu (1979). Etudes sur le Phylloxera vastatrix, Mem, ***Acad. Sci., Paris*** 26: 163-175, 328, 339-341.

Coync, D.L; Plowright, R.A., Twumsi, J and Hunt, D.J.H (1999) Prevalenceof plant parasitic nematodes accociated with rice in

Ghanna with a discussion of their importance. Nematology, 1: 399-405.

Dangar, D.S; Gupta, D.C. and Jain R.K. (1996). Studies on aqueous extract of different parts of *Tagetes erecta* on hatching, larval penetration of *M. javanica*. ***Indian J. Nematol.*** 26 (1): 46-51.

Das, J. and Das, A.K. (2000). Prevalence of root knot nematode of vegetable crops in Assam & Arunachal Pradesh. ***Indian J. Nematol.*** 30 (2): 244-245.

Das, S.N.; Mishra, C.D. and Mahanty, K.C. (1979). Occurence and host preference of some plant parasitic nematodes on pulse crops. ***Indian J. Nematol.***19 (1): 74.

Dastur, J.F. (1936). A nematode disease of rice in the central provinces. ***Proc. Indian. Acad. Sci.*** 108-122.

Deepak Sharma-Poudyal, Ramesh R Pokharel, Sundar M Shrestha and GB Khatri-Chhetri2004). Evaluation of Common Nepalese Rice Cultivars Against Rice Root Knot Nematode, ***Nepal Agric. Res.*** J, 5: 33-36.

De Man, J.G. (1884). Die frie in der reinen Erd un in sussen wasser lebenden Nematoden der nieder land ischen Fauna. ***L ciden Brill.*** 206 pp.

Devrajar, K. (2001). Occurence and distribution of parasitic nematodes in Tanirabarani river basin of Tamil Nadu. ***Indian J. Nematol.*** 31 (2): 175-176.

Devakumar, C. (1994), Nematicidal principles of plant origin. In nematode pest management of crops. D.S. Bhalto and R.K. Walia (eds), *CBS **Publishers, Delhi** PP. 165-189.*

Dhanachand, Ch. (1982). A list of soil inhabiting and plant parasitic nematodes of Manipur. ***Orient Zool.*** (1982) 2: 87-94.

Eisenback, J.D. and Hirschmann, H. (1979). Morphological comparision of second stage juveniles of six populations of Meloidogyne hapla by Sem. ***J. Nematol.*** *II*: 5-16.

Eisenback, J.D, and Triantaphyllous, A.C. (1991). Root knot nematode Meloidogyne species and races. ***Manual of Agricultural Nematology (w.R.Nickle, ed) Marcel Dekker, New York, USA:*** pp 191-274.

Gokte, N., Maheshwari, M.L.& Mathur, U.K. (1991). Nematicidal activity of few essential oils against root knot and cyst nematode species. Indian Journal of nematode Species. ***Indian Journal of Nematology*** 21: 123-127.

Golden, A.M. and Birchfield, w. (1965). *M. gramnicola* (Heteroderidae) a new species of root knot nematode from grass. ***Proc.Helminthol. Soc. Wash***, 32: 228-231.

Gitanjali Devi and NS Azad Thakur., (2007). Screening of Rice Germplasm/Varieties for resistance against root-knot nematode (*Meloidogyne graminicola). Indian journal of Nematology. 37: 1*

Ghorbani, R, wilcock son, s; koochek, A, leifert, C.92008). Soil management for sustainable crop disease control*: a review, environment chemistry letters; 6: 149-162.*

Haseeb, A. And Pandey, R. (1987). Incidence of root knot nematode in medicinal and aromatic plants-new host records. ***Nematropica.*** 17: 209-212.

Hirschmann, H. (1985). The classification of the family Meloidogynidae In: An advanced Treatise on *Meloidogyne* Vol I. Edited by ***U.S.A. North california State University Graphics***. 35-45.

Hussey, R.S. and Janssen, J.G.W (2002). In Plant Resistance to parasitic nematodes (J.L. starr, R. Cook and J. Bridge.eds) CAB, ***International, Wellingford Oxon, U.K.***

Hussey, R.S. and Bakerr, K.R. (1973). A comparison of method of collecting inocula for *Meloidogyne* sepcies including a new technique. *Plant disease report 57: 1025-1028.*

Haider, M.G. and T.H. Askary (2011). Management of plant parasiric nematode through botanicals and growth of sugercane. *Ann. Pl. Protec. Sci.* 19: 433-436.

Hena, H.D. Tiwari, Madhavi Pathak, K. Dwivedi, N.A. Ansari and J.P. Tiwari (2009). Nematicidal effect of angiospermic medicinal plants against *Meloidogyne incognita* on brinjal. *Ann. Pl. Protec. Sci.* **17**: 272-273.

Israel P. and Rao Y.S., (1971). Isolation of sources for nematode resistance in rice. SABRAO, *Newsletter, 3 (1):* 7-10.

Isman, M.B. (2000) Plant essential oil for pest and disease management crop protection, *19: 603-608.*

Jain, R.K., Mathur, K.N. & Singh, R.V. (2007). Estimation of losses due to Plant Parasitic Nematodes on Different Crops in India. ***Indian Journal of Nematology*** 37: 23-25.

Jackai, L, W.N, Inang, E.E & NW obi, (1992. The potential for controlling post flowering pest of cow pea using neem, *Azadirachta indica.* A. Juss, TROPICAL PEST MANAGEMENT, 38: 56-60.

Jairajpuri, M.S. (1962). On a new nematode Boleodorus indicus n. sp. from soil around the roots of onions, ***Allium cepa, Z. Parasitink*** 22: 214-216.

Jairajpuri, M.S. (1964). Studies on Nygellidae, Fam & Belondiridae Thorne, 1939 (Nematoda: Dorylaimoidea) with description of ten new species from India. ***Proc. Helminth. Soe Wash***. 31: 173-187.

Jairajpuri, M.S. (1965). Studies on Dorylaimellus Cobb, 1913 and Nygellus Thorne, 1939 (Nematoda: Dorylaimoidea) with description of three new species ***Nematologica 11***: 207-212.

Jairajpuri, M.S. (1966). A redefinition of Psilenchus De Man 1921 and *Tylenchus* subgenus Filenchus Andrassy, 1954 with the erection of Clavilenchus n. sub genus under Tylenchus bastian, 1865. ***Nematologica 11***: 619-622.

Jairajpuri, M.S. (1967). Qudsiellia gracilis n. gen. n.sp. (nematode: Dorylaimida) from Andamans. ***Indian Nematologica***. 12: 587-590.

Jairajpuri, M.S. and Baqri, Q.H. (1991). Nematode pest of rice. ***Mohan premlani for oxford and IBH publishing Co. Pvt. 66 Janpath, New Delhi***-66pp.

Joymati, L. & Dhanachand, Ch. (1996). Occurence of root knot nematode ***M. incognita*** (Kofoid & White, 1919) Chitwood, 1949, on two medicinal plants – New host record. ***Current Nematology***. (1996) 7 (1): 81-82.

Joymati, L. & Dhanachand, Ch. (1998). Studies on effect of aqueous extracts of Vitex trifolia on ***Meloidogyne incognita*** parasitizing host plant tomato. ***Vasundhara 3***: 60-62.

Joymati, L. & Dhanachand, Ch. (2000). Efficacy of oil extracts of different medicinal plants against root-knot nematode on soybean. ***Vasundhara*** 5: 11-16.

Joymati, L., Mema, W. and Bhanu, Y. (2005). Host range study of root knot nematode in Manipur. ***Indian J. Environ. & Ecoplan*** 10 (3): 102-104.

Joymati, L. (2006). Efficacy of dry power of *Adhatoda vesica* as soil amendment against root knot nematode on brinjal. ***Indian J. Nematol***. 36 (2): 312-314.

Joymati, L. (2007). Effect of essential oil products of some indigenous medicinal plants on egg hatching and larval mortality of *Meloidogyne incognita*. ***Indian J. Nematol***. 37 (2): 176-178.

Joymati, L. (2008). Evaluation of Chloroform methanol extracts of different medicinal plants on egg hatching and larval mortality of ***M. incognita***. ***Indian J. Nematol.*** 38. (2), 168-171.

Joymati, L. (2009). Pathogenecity of root knot nematode ***Meloidogyne incognita*** on two different indigenous crops of Manipur. ***Indian J. Nematol***. 39 (2): 122-125.

Joymati, L. (2009). Effect of Chloroform methanol extracts of different medicinal plants n egg hatching and larval mortality of ***M. incognita***. ***Annals Pl. Protec Sci*** 17 (2): 434-436.

Joymati, L. (2010). Evaluation of Petroleum ether extracts of some Medicinal Plants against root knot nematode on Brinjal. ***Journal of Experimental Sciences Vol. 1, Issue 10***, Pages 20-22.

Joymati, L. (2010). Evaluation of Chloroform methanol extracts of medicinal plants on egg hatching and larval mortality of ***M. incognita. Indian J. Nematol.*** 40 (1): 103-106.

Joymati, L., Romabati, N. & Dhanachand. Ch. (1999). Distribution of host range studies of *M. incognita* (Kofoid and White, 1929) Chitwood, 1949 in medicinal plants of Manipur, Part-I. ***Indian J. Nematol.* 19 (I)**: 79-80.

Joymati, L, Ronibala, Kh, Zenith, Ng and Purnima, (2013), Community analysis of plant parasite nematodes associated with rice in Imphal East district of Manipur (Pourabi*) India. J. Nemalel Vol 43 (1) 109-111.*

Khan, I, A, sayed, M, Shaukat, s.s. and Handoo, Z.A. (2008). Efficacy of four plant extracts on nematodes associated with papaya in sindh, *Pakistan, nematologia mediterranea, 36: 96-98.*

Khan, M.R, Jain, R.K, Singh, R.V. and Pramanle, A (2010) Economically important plant parasitic Nematodes Distribution Atlas, Directorate of Information& Publication of Agriculture, ***Indian council of Agricultural Research, Krishi Anusadhan Bhavan, New delhi, India*** 145PP.

Khan, Matiyar R, Nagesh, M & Khan, M.R. (2012b) Nematodes infestation in horticultural crops, In: Nematode infestation Part-III Horticultural Crops, M.R. Khan & M.S. Jairaipuri (eds) *National Academy of Sceince, India, Allahbad, pp-498-442.*

Khan, A.A. & Khan, M.W. (1996). Distribution of root-knot nematode species and races infesting vegetable crops in eastern Uttar Pradesh. ***Indian Journal of Nematology*** 26: 238-244.

Khan, M.A. & I.A. Wangar (2000). Alleviation of salinity enforced dormancy in atriplex griffthii Moq. Var. stocksii Boiss. ***Seed Science & Technology,*** 28: 29-37.

Kalita M and PN Phukan. (1990). Reactions of some rice cultivars to *Meloidogyne graminicola. Indian J. Nematol.* 20: 215-216.

Kamalwanshi, R.S., Ganguly, S. and Mishra, S.D. (2002). *Indian Journal of Nematology*. **32**: 222.

Kumar, Vinod, R.V. Singh and H.S. Singh (2011). Management of *Meloidogyne incognita* Race 1 and *Rotylenchulus reniformis* by seed treatment with bio-agents, organic cakes and pesticides on cowpea. *Ann. Pl. Protec. Sci.***19**: 164-167.

Lella, N.K., Khan, R.M., Reddy, P.P. & Nidiry, E.S.J. (1992). Nematicidal activity of essential oils of *Pelargonium gravelens* against root knot nematode. ***Nematologia Mediterranea*** 20: 57-58.

Lorenzana OJ, PP Matamis, CB Mallinin, OL Jose and DS De-leon. (1998). Cultural management practices to control rice root knot nematode. Philippine Council for Agriculture, Forestry and Natural Resources Research and Development, Los Banos, Laguna (Philippines). 120p

Meijneke, CAR and Oostenbrink, M (1958), *Tagetes sp* bestriding van altjesaantastingen. *Meded Dir Tunip 21: 283-290.*

Muhammad S., Suberru H.A., Amusa N.A. Agaji M.D. (2001). The effect of soil amendment with saw dust & rice husks on the growth & incidence of seedling blight of *Tamarrindus indica* Linn caused by *Macrophomina phaseolina* and *Rhizoctonia solani*. ***Moor J. Agric. Res*** **2**: 40-46.

Naidu, P.H., Haritha, v, Sudheer, M.J and Prasad, J.S. (2007). Identification of root knot nematode *M. incognita* race prevailing in chittor District of Andhra Pradesh. Indian J. Nematode.37: 107-108.

Netcher, C., and R.A. Sikora (1990). Nematode parasites of vegetables. P. 251 in M. Luc. A.R. Sikora & J. Bridge eds. Plant parasitic nematodes in sub-tropical & tropical agriculture. ***CAB International, Wallingford, U.K.***

Nidiry, E.S.J.; Chandravadana, M.V.; Khan, R.M. and Rac. M.S. (1994). In vitro nematicidal activity of the extracts of bulbs and seeds of onion against root knot nematode ***M. incognita***. ***Nematol Medit***. 22: 37-40.

Norton, D.C. (1978). Some simple methods of community analysis. In: Ecology of Plant Parasitic Nematodes. ***John Willey & Sons, New York***. pp. 66-68.

Orton, W.K.J. (1973). *Meloidogyne incog*nita CIH description of plant parasitic nematodes Set 2. No. 18. ***Farnham Royal U.K. commonwealth Agricultural Bureaux.***

Olabiyi, T.I., (2008) Pathogenecity study and Nemathotoxic properties of some plant extracts on the root knot nematode pest of Tomato, *Lycopersicon escalentum*. Plant pathology journal, *7 (1) 45-49.*

Pankaj, H.K. Sharma, H.K., Khajan Singh and Jagan lal (2010). Incidence of rice root knot nematode *M. graminicola* in rice nursery in Gautam Budh Nagar and Bulandsharh districts of Uttar Pradesh. Indian J. Nematol, 40: 247-249

Pankaj, A; Sirohi, R.K; Jain and K. Singh (2011). Incidence of *M. graminicola* on rice in Andaman islands. Ann.Pl.Protec.Sci., 19: 259-260.

Pandey.R. (1990). Studies on Phytonematotoxic properties in the extracts of some medicinal and aromatic plants. ***Int. Nematol. Network. Newsl.*** 7 (3): 19-20.

Phukan, P.N. (1995). Nematode problem of rice crops in India IV. Stem nematode anb rice root knot nematode In: Nematode pest management an appraised of ecofriendly approaches (G. Swarup, D.R. Dasgupta and Gill J.S.eds). Nematological society of India, New-Delhi, India, pp.156-160.

Prasad, D., D. Ram and Imtiaz Ahmad (2002). Managemant of plant parasitic nematodes by the use of botanicals. Ann. Pl. Protec. Sci.**10**: 360-364.

Patel, S.S., N.K. Verma, C. Catterjee and K. Gauthaman (2010). Screening of *Caesalpinia pulcherrima* Linn flowers for analgesic and anti-inflammatory activities. ***Int. J. Applied Res. Nat. Prod., 3***: 1-5.

Perez M. P., J.A. Navas, M.J Pascual & P. Castillo (2003). Nematicidal activity of essential oils and organic amendments from Asteraceae against root knot nematodes. ***Plant Pathology 52***, 395-401

Phukan, P.N. and Sanwal, K.C. (1979). Taxonomic studies on nematodes from Assam, Indian (Paratylenchidae: Tylenchida). ***Indian J. Nematol***. 9 (1): 20-26.

Phukan, P.N. and Sanwal, K.C. (1980). Two new species of *Aglenchus* and record of *Cephalenchus leptus* (Tylenchidae: Nematoda) from Assam. ***Indian J. Nematol.*** 10 (I): 28-34.

Phukan, P.N. and Sanwal, K.C. (1980a). Two new species of *Macroposthonia* De Man, 1880 (Criconematidae: Nematoda) from Assam. ***Indian J. Nematol. 10***: 135-140.

Pimentel, D., Hepperly, P., J., Douds, D and Seidel, R (2005). Environmental, energetic and economic comparision of organic and conventional farming systems. Bio Science 55: 573-582.

Prakash A. & Rao, J. (1997). Botanical pesticides in agriculture. CRC, Lewis ***Publishers, Boca Raton, New York, London, Tokyo***, 461pp.

Prasad, J.S; Panwar, M.S and Rao, Y.S. (1985). Occurrence of the root knot nematode *M. graminicola* in semi deep water rice. Current science, 54: 387-388.

Pankaj, A; Sirohi, R.K; Jain and K. Singh (2011). Incidence of *M. graminicola* on rice in Andaman islands. Ann.Pl.Protec.Sci., 19: 259-260.

Pokharel, R.R. (2009) Damage of root knot nematode (*M. graminicola*) to rice in fields with different soil types ***Nematologia Mediterranea*** 37: 203-217.

Plow right R, Bridge J. (1990). Effect of *M. graminicola* (nematode) on the establishment, growth and yield of rice ***C.V.IR.36, Nematol***, 36: 81-89.

Quencherve, P.; Drop, F and Topart, P. (1995). Host status some weeds to *Meloidogyne* spp. Pratylenchus spp., Helicotylenchus spp. and *Rotylenchulus reniformis* associated with vegetable cultivated in polytunnels in Martinique. ***Nematropica***. 24 (2): 119-157.

Rautary. B.N.; Mohapatra, M.P. and Das, S.N. (1987). Effects of *Meloidogyne incognita* on ginger Zingiber officinale Rose. ***Indian J. Nematol***. 17 (2) 327-328.

Rathour, K.S., Sharma, s and Ganguly, s (2003). Phytonematode Communities associated with perennial ornamental and medicinal plants in Bareilly District, Uttar Pradesh, pp 31-38, In: ***Proceedings of National symposium on Biodiversity & Management of nematode cropping system of sustainable Agriculture, Jaipur, India***.

Rathour, K.S, Dubey, J and Ganguly, S. (2010) Documentation of plant parasitic and beneficial soil nematodes & their communities in Madhya Pradesh India, ***Indian J. Nematol*** 40: 66-73.

Ravichandra, N.G, Krishnappa, K and Reddy B.M.R (2003). Occurence & distribution of Phyto parasitic nematode associated with rice in Mandya district Karnataka. Indian J. Nematol 33-178.

Rao, Y.S. and Biswas, H. (1973) Evaluation of field losses in rice due to the root knot nematode. Indian J. Nematology 3: 74.

Raveendran, V. and Nadakal, A.M. (1975). An additional list of plant infected by the root knot nematode, *Meloidogyne incognita* (Kofoid and White, 1919) Chitwood, 1949. ***Indian J. Nematol***. 5: 126-127.

Reddy, P.P.; Setty, K.G.H. and Govindee, H.C. (1972). Susceptibility of flu cured tobacco variety NC-95 to southern root knot nematode. ***Mysore J. Agric Sci***. 6: 192-193.

Reddy, P.P. and Singh, D, B. (1979). Nematode problems of citrus in India. ***PANS. 25***: 409-419.

Reddy, P.P. (1984). Efficacy of seed treatment with nematicides for the control of *M. incognita* infecting, french bean and peas. ***Indian J. Nematol*** 14 (1): 39-40.

Rao Y.S.& Israel (1973). Life history & bionomics of *M. gramnicola*, the rice root knot nematode. Ind. Phytopathol 26: 333-340.

Roy A.K., (1973). Reaction of some rice cultivars to the attack of *Meloidogyne graminicola. Indian Journal of Nematology,* 3: 72-73.

Sahu, R., Chandra, p. and Poddar, A.n. (2011) Community analysis of plant parasitic nematodes prevalent in Vegetable crops in district Durg of Chhattisgarh. India.Res.J.Parasitol.6: 83-89

Sampath S., Rao Y.S. and Roy J.K., (1970). The nature of pest resistance in an indica rice variety TK M6. Current Science, 39 (7): 162-163.

Sasser, J.N. (1979). Root knot Nematodes (*Meloidogyne species*) Systematics, Biology and Control. (eds.) Lamberti, F and Taylor, ***C.E. Azad press***. pp. 359-373.

Sasser, J.N. (1980). Root-Knot nematodes: a global menace to crop production. ***Pl. Dis.*** 64 (1): 36-41.

Sasser, J.N.; Carter, C.C. and Taylor, A.L. (1982). A guide to the development of plant nematology program. ***IMP publication. North Carolina State University, Raleigh***. 221.

Sasser, J.N. & Carter, C.C. (1985). An advanced Treatise on *Meloidogyne* Vol. 1., Biology and Control (Edn.). ***International Meloidogyne Project***.

Sasser, J.N. & Kirkpatrik, T.L. (1982). Efficacy of avermectins for root knot control in tobacco. ***Plant Dis.*** 66: 961-65.

Sen, K and Dasgupta, M.K. (1975). Further report on the occurrence of *Meloidogyne* spp. On some plants in West Bengal including a few new host records from India. ***Indian J. Nematol***. 5: 128-129.

Sen, K and Dasgupta, M.K. (1977). Additional host of the root knot nematode *Meloidogyne* spp. from ***India. J. Nematol***. 7 (1): 74.

Schmutterer, (1990). Properties and potential of natural pesticides for the neem tree, *Azadirachta indica. Annual review Entomology 35: 271-298.*

Sidddiqui, I.A. & Taylor, D.P. (1969). Feeding mechanism of Aphelenchoides bicaudatus on three fungi and an alga. ***Nematologic***a 15: 503-509.

Siddiqui, M.R. (1959). Studies on *Xiphinema* spp. (Nematoda: Dorylaimoidea) From Aligarh (North India), with comments on the genus *Longidorus micoletzky*, 1922. ***Proc. Helminth. Soc. Wash.*** 26: 151-163

Siddiqui, M.R. (1961). Studies on species of Criconematinae (Nematoda: Tylenchida) from India. ***Proc. Helminth. Soc. Washington*** 28: 19-34.

Siddiqui, M.R. (1963). Four new species in the sub-family Tylenchinae (Nematoda) from North. ***India. Z. Parasitkde***. 23: 397-404.

Siddiqui, M.R. (1964). Four new species in the family Belondiridae (nematode: Dorylaimida). ***Labdev. J. Sci. Tech***. 2: 37-41.

Siddiqui, M.R. (1965). Five new species in the family Belondiridae (Nematoda: Dorylaimida). ***Labdev. J. Sci Tech***. 2: 37-41.

Siddiqui, M.R. (1978). The unusual position of the phasmida in *Coslenchus costatus* (de Man, 1912) gen. n. and order Tylenchida (nematode: Tylenchida). ***Nematologica.*** 24: 449-450.

Siddiqui, M.R. (1986). Tylenchida, Parasites of Plants and Insects, Wallingford, ***UKCAB International***, IX - 645pp.

Siddiqui, Z.A.; Rashid, A; Farooqi, N and Bisheya, F (1987). A Survey of plant parasitic nematodes associated with citrus in Libya and trials on chemical control. ***Indian J. Nematol***. 17 (1): 76-83.

Singh, P.P. (1988). Chemical control of *Meloidogyne incognita* in tomato nursery. ***Indian Journal of Horticulture*** 45: 166-168.

Singh, R.S. (1965). Control of root-knot of tomato with organic soil amendment. ***Fao Plant Prot. Bull.*** 13: 35-37.

Singh, I, Gaur, H.S. Brar, S.S. Sharma, S.K. & Sakheya, Pk (2003) *International Journal of Nematolozy 13: 79-86.*

Singh, N, Gill, J.S and krishnanda, N. (1979) Prevelence of root knot nematode in Nilgeri hills *Indian Phytopathol.*32: 499-501.

Sinha, S.C. (1996). Medicinal plants of Manipur. Mass and Sinha, ***Manipur Association for Science and Society (MASS).*** 238pp.

Singh A, Singh D.K. (2001) Molluscicidal activity of Lawsonia inermis & its binary & tertiary combination with other plant derived molluscicides. ***India J. Exp. Bid. 2001 Mar, 39 (3):*** 263-268.

Sharma. PoudyalD, R.R. Pokharel, S.M. Shrestha and G.B. Khatri Chetri (2002). Population and effect of rice root knot nematode in diseased and healthy looking rice plants and their distribution in field. J. Inst. Agric. Anim. Sci.23: 9-14.

Singh, I., Gaur, H.S., Briar, S.S., Sharma, S.K. and Sakhuja, P.K. (2003). *International Journal of Nematology*. **13**: 79-86.

Southey, J.F. (1986). Laboratory methods for work with plant and soil nematodes. ***London Univ. Agric. Fish. Food H.M.S.O.***, 202.

Stripe, F, PessionBazzi, A, Lorenzoni, E, Strochi, P, Montanaro, L, Sperti, S (1976) Studies on the proteins from the seeds of *Croton tigilium* and *Jatropha curcas*. Biochemistry Journal156: 16.

Supratoyo (1993) studies on the effect of *T. erecta & T. patula* for controlling plant parasite nematodes on banana. *IImu pertanian 5: 681-691.*

Taylor, A.l., Sasser, J.N. & Nelson, L. A. (1982). Relationship of climate and soil characteristic to geographical distribution of *Meloidogyne* species in Agriculturc soil crop. ***Publ. Dept. Plant Path. North Carolina State Univ. and U.S. Agency Int. Dev Raleigh N*** C 65p.

Trivedi; P.C.; Sharma, C and Datta, S (1986). New host record of the root knot nematode *M. incognita* (Kofoid and White, 1919) Chitwood, 1949. ***Indian J. Nematol.*** 16 (2): 279.

Trudgill, DL, Block VC.2001. Apomictic, polyphagous root knot nematode exceptionally successfully & damaging biotrophic root pathogen. Ann. Rev. *Phytopathol. 39: 53-77.*

Verma, R.R. and Singh, H.R. (1983). Distribution and host records of root-knot nematode *Meloidogye* spp. In Garhwal hills. ***Indian J. Nematol.*** 13: 234.

Villanueva, L.M., Prot, J.C. and Matias D.M. (1992). Plant parasitic nematodes associated with upland rice in the phillipines. Journal of plant protectionTropics.

Webster, J.M. (1972). ***Economic Nematology Academic Press, New York***, pp. 563.

Whitehead, A.G. (1968). Taxonomy of *Meloidogyne* (Nematoda: Heteroderidae) with description of four new species. ***Trans. Zool. Soc. Land.*** 31: 263 – 401.

Wink M., (2008) Plant secondary metabolism: Diversity, function & its evolution. ***Natural product communication 3 (8):*** 1205-1216.

Yujioka, Nacar, S, puteiusky, E, Ravid, U, Yaniv, Zand Spiegel, Y (2000). Nematicidal activity of essential oils and their components against the root knot nematode. ***J. Phytopathology*** 90 (7): 710-715.

Yik, C.P.& Birchfield, W (1979). Host studies and reactions of cultivars to *M. gramnicola*. ***J. Phytopathology***, 69: 497-499.

www.ingramcontent.com/pod-product-compliance
Ingram Content Group UK Ltd.
Pitfield, Milton Keynes, MK11 3LW, UK
UKHW041852190726
13854UKWH00002B/847

9 798885 467353